Historic Taverns of Boston

Historic Taverns of Boston

370 years of tavern history in one definitive guide

Gavin R. Nathan

iUniverse, Inc.
New York Lincoln Shanghai

Historic Taverns of Boston
370 years of tavern history in one definitive guide

iUniverse books may be ordered through booksellers or by contacting:

iUniverse
2021 Pine Lake Road, Suite 100
Lincoln, NE 68512
www.iuniverse.com
1-800-Authors (1-800-288-4677)

ISBN-13: 978-0-595-39370-1 (pbk)
ISBN-13: 978-0-595-83766-3 (ebk)
ISBN-10: 0-595-39370-5 (pbk)
ISBN-10: 0-595-83766-2 (ebk)

Printed in the United States of America

I dedicate this book to my Mother & Father who introduced me to old taverns in England, which sparked a lifelong passion. In addition were it not for the support of Beth and her work in structural historic restoration in Boston, this book would not exist.

All profits from the sale of this book are donated to PreservatiON MASS, the only statewide, private non-profit preservation organization dedicated to preserving the Commonwealth's historic and cultural heritage. Today, PreservatiON MASS works in partnership with national, state and local preservation organizations and individuals across the Commonwealth to preserve our heritage. Helping threatened resources through their Ten Most Endangered Historic Resources Program and through working with the many concerned individuals who identify neglected/threatened structures in their communities.

Special thanks go to all those who helped me at the Boston Public Library, National Park Service, The Bostonian Society, Golden Ball Tavern in Weston, PreservatiON MASS, Society for Protection of New England Antiquities, Suffolk County Probate Records, Museum of Fine Arts, Jamaica Plain Historical Society, Boston Beer Company, Barleycorn and the many local bar owners and brewers who contributed to this book.

“There is nothing which has yet been contrived by man
which so much happiness is produced
as by a good tavern or inn.”

Dr. Samuel Johnson (1709–1784)

Contents

List of Illustrations

FOREWORD

Boston taverns in the 1700's were so abundant visitors commented that every other house in Boston was a tavern. The question has to be asked what remains of these mecca's of hospitality today? Gavin R. Nathan tackles the subject from two fronts, combining new research of Boston's current entertainment scene with historical insights. The result is a 'then and now' perspective that ties the past to the present by addressing 370 years of rich tavern history in one book. Until now, very little had been written about Boston's old inns and ordinaries. Gavin sets the record straight by collating evidence to catalogue every known tavern that existed from 1630 to 1830. The result, *Historic Taverns of Boston* is a very significant contribution to our understanding of old taverns in America.

The history of Boston itself cannot be written without reference to taverns. The important role of taverns in key historical events such as the Boston Tea Party, the Battle of Bunker Hill and Paul Revere's ride is unearthed here in detail. Boston taverns were an institution in their own right. The reader of this book will discover what happened when this institution came into contact with others in the local community, namely the Church, the Courts and a famous university. For the first time the relevance and importance of early Boston taverns in American history becomes clear to all.

The historical picture is completed with a thorough investigation into the architecture, decoration, music and entertainment that were common in these old taverns. A wealth of information is unearthed on the most popular and most bizarre beverages, and how to create these authentic drinks today. Gavin mined original recipes and culinary research to create a typical tavern menu that dismisses a popular delusion that puritan food and drink was bland and boring. The recipes selected are anything but, infusing native ingredients with spices from around the world.

In successfully linking the past to the present the author provides an update on Boston's current tavern scene and the local brewing industry. This research alone makes *Historic Taverns of Boston* the most comprehensive 'off the beaten path' guide to Boston taverns today. There are one or two hidden tavern treasures that even local experts will be surprised to discover. For the out-of-towner, many of the recommendations and comprehensive listings of current taverns are enough to fill a week with tavern trekking in and around Boston.

The work is both a significant historical contribution and an essential guide to help locals and visitors get the most out of Boston taverns.

A.S., Brewer & Bar Critic, Boston

Preface

I'm English, a *Red Coat* or *Limey* as the locals call me. My parents raised me in a small town called Benfleet in Essex, near London, England. I grew up in an environment where pubs (Public Houses) serve as social centers, places where family and friends meet and new friendships are established. Generation after generation, a family patronizes the same pubs. Great effort is put into preserving their history and authenticity and little has changed in these pubs since they were built, in some cases as far back as the 1600's. Public houses have played a role throughout my life. Just after I was born my parents took me to meet friends at a local pub. At the age of 14 I was going there alone and by 16 I was ordering my own drinks. By the time I reached 19 years of age I was fortunate enough to work in a local pub as a bartender. By 21 they entrusted me with the keys. When I left home and moved to London I spent my weekends visiting old inns, sampling their fare and understanding their past. As time went by my interest in old taverns grew.

Arriving in Boston on a harsh winter's day, I sought the refuge of a pub to escape from the piercing wind. The nearest place was an Irish bar. I washed down a bowl of tasty clam chowder with a pint of Sam Adams by the log fire. I remember pondering how my ancestors, whom I had followed across the Atlantic, would have quenched their thirst and appetite as they came ashore in Boston? And so the seed was first planted to grow my understanding of Boston taverns. As I began this research I soon discovered, with some disappointment, that people had done little over time to preserve the heritage of Boston taverns. Nearly all the original bars and their buildings had disappeared, and information on their existence was far from accessible.

Since taverns played such a large role in my life in England, it's no wonder I felt so compelled to write this book. The objective is to capture the importance of taverns in Boston's history and to help people appreciate what tavern life was really like in colonial times. My quest to discover the heritage of Boston's taverns took me into a world where pirates and politicians rubbed shoulders at the bar, in taverns that doubled as courthouses, constabularies, libraries and post offices. Where people drank *punch*, *flip*, *grog* and *syllabub* while celebrating ordinations or plotting to overthrow the British. A handful of Boston taverns have secured their place in history books, credited with helping to shape America into what it is today. Some local taverns have left their legacy on the surrounding area in terms of street names, business names and several plaques. Through my research I unearthed places in Boston today that have managed to preserve pieces of tavern history that are enough to spark the imagination of people in times gone by.

This book also contains carefully selected food and drink recipes to help the reader recreate authentic colonial tavern fare including bizarre drink concoctions enjoyed by our Founding Fathers. I could not write and recommend something I had not experienced, so all these colonial recipes have been personally tried and tested by the author. Many of my guests have had the pleasure of sampling drinks unheard of today and to my surprise they have been more than politely happy with the results. Likewise, I hope you enjoy creating the drink recipes in this book, but watch out; some are stronger than others and a few are particularly potent.

Throw out your preconceptions of Boston history, based on powdered wigs, curled up shoes and quill penned declarations. Instead, get ready to explore a piece of Boston's past and present that your history teacher will have overlooked.

Cheers!
Gavin Nathan

NOTES

Notes on Front Cover Design:

The **pineapple** image seen on the back page and frontispiece is of great significance to local taverns. The association between taverns and pineapples began when sea captains would return to the colony with fruits, spices, and rum gathered during their travels. The captain would spear a pineapple on a fence post outside his house to signify his safe return to friends and neighbors. The pineapple served as an invitation for people to visit, sample the exotic food and drink, while listening to tales of faraway lands. Colonial tavern keepers adopted the pineapple in advertising their business. At inns throughout New England the top of bedposts were carved into pineapples. Even today pineapples are still used in signs at local hotels and restaurants.

Notes on Preface:

'Red Coat' originates from the English tradition of wearing a very noticeable Red on the battlefield, to the delight of the local militia. Englishmen also acquired the nickname 'Limey' from the limes they would suck on, for Vitamin C, to prevent scurvy while crossing the Atlantic.

The Evolution of Boston Taverns

FLOORBOARDS creak underfoot as you walk in. A blazing fire in the colossal hearth warms the candlelit room. Travelers relax on worn wooden benches, sipping from polished pewter mugs while enjoying wild game, chowders and preserves…at least this is the image of old taverns people like to believe, the epitome of good old-fashioned American hospitality. However it took nearly a hundred years for early American taverns to develop this level of sophistication. To understand how these places evolved in Boston we must explore how settlers carried a need and love of beer from their homeland, England, to New England.

Before Taverns, Came Beer

THE Arbella set sail from England in March 1630, the flagship of a fleet of fourteen vessels with eight hundred and forty passengers comprising the Massachusetts Bay Colony. Under the leadership of John Winthrop, the fleet left England with "40 tuns" of beer (about 10,000 gallons) for the arduous journey. They chose beer because it kept well at sea, while water fouled in wooden barrels. A cooper was even on hand to ensure casks were kept tight. Although they did not realize it at the time, ale had prevented the dreaded scurvy during their journey across the Atlantic. Wisdom of the day advised that alcohol was essential to remain in good health; a tipple warmed you on a cold night, kept fevers at bay, made hard work bearable, assisted with digestion and created a general well being. On land as well as sea, ale was considered safer than water. Since much of the water supply was polluted in 17th century Europe, the Puritans expected the same situation in their new land. Beer was such a necessity that a successful brewer called Richard Tuffneale, was invited to be a founding investor of the Massachusetts Bay Company which commissioned the *Arbella*.

Winthrop's fleet reached the shores of Massachusetts in mid-July of 1630. Their first landing at Salem was disappointing; the settlement was short of food (and beer) and unable to support the fleet. The *Arbella* continued its journey, finally landing at the mouth of the Charles River, Charlestown, where they decided to stay. By then the Puritans' health had deteriorated due to what was known as the General Sickness (exposure, scurvy, pneumonia etc.). Beer was rationed to ensure there was enough for those who really needed it. Across the

Charles River, William Blackstone, a former clergyman, was living an isolated existence as a trapper. Indian friends told him of the dire situation his fellow countrymen were facing. Blackstone sent a message to John Winthrop, advising him that the Trimountain Hills on his side of the river were far more suitable for habitation. Three months later, many of the settlers had moved from Charlestown and the new settlement was called Boston after its English namesake in the County of Lincolnshire. Over the next few years many more Lincolnshire migrants arrived, including 250 from Boston itself. These Englishmen dearly loved their beer and could not rely on intermittent supplies from England. Puritan women, (known as "alewives" because they brewed beer), soon incorporated brewing into their household routines making beer a dietary staple. One of the first additions to their primitive dwellings was a brew house or alehouse; built on the side of their homes to remove the heat and potential fire hazard of brewing away from the kitchen.

Nutritionally, alcoholic beverages supported a healthy population at a time when people believed that drinking water would make you ill, from diseases such as tuberculosis. Despite being surrounded by a plentiful supply of pristine water, far less water was consumed in those days. Beer was considered a much safer bet. Brewing beer involved heating water, thereby neutralizing many of the harmful bacteria it could contain. Also, by converting their grain to beer, apples to cider, pears to perry and honey to mead, early settlers were able to preserve liquids without refrigeration. The average colonial consumed an unbelievable 3.1 gallons of liquids such as beer, hard cider, perry and mead weekly. This quantity of liquid equates to 6000 calories per day compared to typical modern day energy requirements of 2000 calories. The large intake can be explained by the more physical work, which required more energy. The beer also provided a distraction from their arduous tasks. In addition, the common practice of preserving meat with salt, made people thirsty, another reason for their larger liquid intake. In any case the paths into the woods must have been well marked.

Several of the early settlers brewed beer for their family and friends, and opened their doors to travelers. These otherwise residential buildings became known as alehouses. Boston's first building dedicated to serving beer and catering for travelers opened its doors in 1633, three years after the *Arbella* arrived. From this point forward the history of Boston cannot be written without reference to taverns. However these early houses of entertainment were strikingly different to the bars in Boston today. Each stage in the evolution of Boston taverns is described in the following paragraphs.

Puritan Ordinaries

In England a meal served with unlimited ale at a fixed price was called an 'ordinary.' Boston taverns were first known as ordinaries. While only a few ordinaries were actually registered during the 1630's, unlicensed premises existed, where the law turned a blind eye until trouble broke out. Boston's first recorded ordinary was Cole's in 1633. Established by Samuel Cole, a comfit (dried sweet fruit and nuts) producer in a prime location near the old docks by Fanuiel Hall Square. The second ordinary or 'house of entertainment' in Boston opened in 1637 by William Baulston, nearby at Dock Square. In the same year Mr. Robert Sedgewick was selected as Captain for Charlestown and promptly issued the first license to brew beer for the Colony. This license was purely a formality as he already established a brewery and had been brewing beer for some time. After Cole's, the next recorded ordinary was Hudson's House in 1640, owned by William Hudson, a baker at the head of Long Wharf. Brewing was often performed alongside baking, so the alehouse was a natural diversification for this baker.

Ordinaries were very basic, often just a room or two in the proprietor's two-story wooden home. The family would live upstairs and run their business downstairs. The atmosphere was more like a coffee shop than the bars of today. The Puritan 'ordinary' provided the warmest welcome a new face in Boston could expect to receive. If you were sick you were nursed, if you were hungry, thirsty, cold, tired, without shelter—whatever your state—the ordinary would rectify it. Ordinaries were not opened purely for the convenience of travelers; they also provided comfort to local townspeople, creating a social forum to exchange news and opinions over refreshment. It was said that if the landlord did not know the news of the day his wife certainly did! Compared to present day bars there was much less bustle, less pressure to consume, less marketing and less show. The landlord (tavern keeper) opened the doors of his house to all. For his guests, in the company of strangers, the ordinary was like a home from home.

As ordinaries rapidly grew in number; their proprietors were required to obtain a license. Cotton Mather, clergyman, teacher and recorder of New England life, said by 1675 "*every other building in Boston is an ale house*". Wandering through Boston streets in 1677 you had by then a choice of 27 establishments. All sold beer but only seven stocked wine, according to census and court records.

Colonial Taverns

By the end of the seventeenth century ordinaries had multiplied and were known as taverns by most people. The word tavern itself is a relation of "*tabernacle*"—a sanctuary, according to the dictionary. By now taverns were firmly established in Boston and, as we shall discover later, ready to play an important role in organizing resistance to rock the world's then greatest power, Britain. By 1756 the number of licensed taverns had reached 156 in Boston. In 1775 Governor Powell made a similar statement as Cotton Mather did 100 years earlier, equally alarmed by the popularity and growth of taverns, he suggested that every other building in Boston appeared to be a house of entertainment. In order to determine if these statements were an exaggeration or an accurate estimate, the author researched court records and census data of the time. Data is available for 1677, 1705, 1737 and 1765, so figures for other years have been extrapolated in the following table:

Year	Licensees	Residents per Tavern
1677	27	115
1696	75	89
1705	70	100
1708	72	111
1710	61	143
1718	74	142
1737	177	96
1740	180	93
1752	162	97
1756	156	110
1758	135	117
1765	134	116

Figure 1: Number of taverns per resident in Boston

If one assumes four people per household, the figure is more like one tavern for every thirty residents than every other household. So both statements above are clearly over-estimates. However, it is interesting to note that the growth in taverns kept pace with the growth in Boston's population; the ratio between taverns and residents remained constant as Boston's population more than quadrupled over the 100 years studied.

Inns for Stages & Houses for Gentlemen

Inns purposely built to accommodate the growth in stagecoach travel to and from Boston mark a new era in Boston's tavern history. The word 'inn', universal in England for describing public houses since the 1600's, was little used in Boston until the late 1700's. At this time inns were developed to cater for more affluent business travelers using the new stagecoach services. These larger establishments sold wine and distilled liquors alongside more common beverages such as ale and cider. As Boston evolved into a very successful trading hub, another variety of taverns emerged, called 'Houses.' Created predominantly for Boston's increasingly affluent upper class. Old mansions, originally the homes of Boston's elite, became victims of urban sprawl as commercialization encroached on their doorstep. These grand dwellings, in what were previously residential areas, were ideal for transformation into more up scale versions of the inns and taverns normally seen in Boston during the 1700's. Originally called 'Houses', they later morphed into hotels, fulfilling demand from an increasingly more affluent genre of business travelers and finally wealthy tourists in the 1800's.

The primary focus of this book is Boston's tavern heyday, comprising the ordinaries and taverns of the 17th and 18th century. Historically significant establishments from the 1800's onwards are mentioned where relevant.

Bars: A Modern Creation

At the turn of the 20th century, Edward Field in 'The Colonial Tavern' concludes by stating "The New England tavern as an institution has vanished, but its importance as an educational factor in the life of New England will remain." Samuel Adams Drake, a local researcher of Boston taverns in the early 1900's, also notes "No words need be wasted upon the present degradation which the name tavern implies to polite ears…now associated with the slums of the city…the tavern has had its day…" Tavern life in Boston changed dramatically from the days of Sam Adams, 18th century patriot, through the life of Sam Adams Drake, 20th century historian. The degradation of taverns is also reflected in their terminology: The word tavern has it roots in providing a refuge (tabernacle), whereas the modern day equivalent 'bar' has its origins in something far less comforting—the barred Dutch doors added to the tavern rooms in the late 18th century to keep the landlord's liquor and money out of reach of his clientele.

Both Drake and Field also complained about the loss of tavern signs. At one time there were few Boston streets where you could not walk without passing under this unique art. Virtually all were removed over time. Nowadays these distinctive wooden signs are making a comeback on Boston streets, many retro designs can be seen in this book. Both Drake and Fields would, no doubt, also be surprised to find out the word tavern is making a comeback. Today bars are capitalizing on their heritage, like the Union Oyster House and Warren Tavern, bearing names that were once lost in time, such as The Green Dragon and Bell in Hand. The word tavern is now gradually being associated with history and preservation, as opposed to the degradation of Boston's inner city as mentioned above. Samuel Adams Drake would be even more surprised to discover his earlier namesake has been turned into an icon of the Boston Brewing Company and successfully exported worldwide.

Are we experiencing a tavern renaissance? Yes. Let's toast to the continued rejuvenation of Boston taverns in the 21st century and the latter sections of this book recommend some good taverns in which to do just that.

AN INSTITUTION

TAVERNS were so woven into the attitudes, traditions and landscape of America they deserve the title of institution. Taverns provided new arrivals to the colony with their first opportunity to socialize, a place where immigrants had their first taste of a new land and took their first steps to becoming Americans. Located at the center of the community and welcome to all (well nearly all), taverns were an institution of the common folk as much as the privileged and wealthy. To the local community, taverns were the malls, motels and restaurants of their era. To traveling merchants, taverns provided a marketplace, conference center, hotel and entertainment complex all rolled into one. Taverns were at the centre of every community; they helped business happen and the colony grow. Inside these bars, ship cargoes and stocks were bought and sold, important announcements posted and new companies organized.

Socially, taverns provided a convenient place for locals to meet and network by sharing experiences over a pint of ale. Such an open environment prompted discussions that helped reinforce social norms in a young and rapidly growing community. Conversations would range from political opinions to arguments over the price of wheat or discussions of the minister's sermon. Dinners were held for fraternities, religious events and political causes. Overnight visitors brought news from other parts of the colony and from overseas, helping Bostonians maintain contact with their mother country and beyond. News was posted on the taproom walls. Politically taverns provided a network of communication that proved invaluable to Sam Adams and other patriots' as we shall discover later. Taverns were an institution in their own right for the social and commercial reasons mentioned here. Next we shall discover what happened when this institution came into contact with other institutions in the local community, namely the Church, the Courts and a famous University.

Bars & Bibles

INDULGENCE and temperance of fermented beverages have been the yin and yang of American society since the first settlers stepped off the boat. Taverns were a necessity to the early pilgrims but conflicted with John Winthrop's, and other Puritan's, ideals for moral health. An intimate relationship ensued for centuries between the religious and the non-religious types of 'meetinghouse' in New England. The relationship is so intertwined over time that John Winthrop's original meetinghouse in Charlestown ironically morphed into a tavern itself, known as the Three Cranes Tavern. The Puritan's ordinary was always close to their church; in fact the positioning of taverns was a strategic decision for local government. In 1651 Boston authorities gave permission for John Vyall (of the Ship Tavern) to open an ordinary as long as he "*keepe it near the new meeting house.*" Most taverns were already located near meetinghouses so that churchgoers chilled during long winter services, or overcome by the heat in summer, could seek refuge and refreshment close by. At noon rest a mug of flip would have no doubt been ideal for raising cheer amongst weary worshippers. Reports exist of people relaxing so much in taverns they became incapacitated for the afternoon service.

Occasional Beers

Special occasions often warranted a special beer. When Reverend Thomas Shepherd of Newtowne, Mass. was ordained head of the church a special ordination beer was brewed for the festivities. Ordination Day was almost as important a day for the tavern as for the meetinghouse. Visiting ministers who assisted in ordinations of a new minister were usually entertained in the local tavern. The owner of Cambridge's first tavern was the deacon of the church, and then Steward of Harvard. Nearby in Fitchburg the local tavern served as the church on Sabbath. In fact more people were probably found in Boston's taverns than churches on a Sunday. This prompted a law in 1656 making drinking illegal on Sabbath. Only in the last hundred years has situating taverns near houses of worship been perceived as undesirable. In many Massachusetts towns laws were later passed to actually prevent the granting of liquor licenses within 500 feet of a church. The warmth and good spirit of the tavern was in competition with the often cold and uncomfortable environment in the church.

Regular consumption of alcohol was accepted, but increasing amounts of drunkard-ness in the new colony led Puritan leaders to associate over-consumption of alcohol with evil. Increase Mather's 'Wo to Drunkards' created in Boston during 1673 is a great example of this; *"Drink is in itself a good creature of God, and to be received with thankfulness, but the abuse of drink is from Satan, the wine is from God, but the Drunkard is from the Devil".*

Liquor & The Law

John Winthrop's model of Christian society needed help from the local government when it came to keeping colonials on church pews and not tavern stools.

Local taverns were regarded as necessary evils, essential for sailors and travelers but not essential for local residents. Church leaders feared people wasting productive hours loitering, singing, dancing, gambling, playing games and drinking. On several occasions the church took their concerns to the General Court of Massachusetts, who governed Boston taverns. The result being that laws were passed on the amount of time townspeople were allowed to stay in taverns during any one visit and the hour they were expected to leave and go home. At one point local consumers were required to buy beer in a "take-out" manner to avoid any perceived loitering in the taverns. Even then, only reputable heads of households were allowed to bring their bottles to the tavern to be filled in the taproom.

Despite various attempts encouraged by the church to stop the growth in taverns, political and commercial interests were far more powerful. By 1675 the number of taverns in Boston was clearly unacceptable by some, Cotton Mather himself noted that 'every other house in Boston' was a tavern. Despite a string of laws, listed in the timeline below, a hundred years later Governor Pownall repeated Cotton's statement. The growth in taverns had more than kept pace with Boston's expansion. The following laws and sentences found in court records, mostly from the General Court of Massachusetts, provide a great insight into early colonial attitudes to taverns and drinking:

1631 The Massachusetts Bay Authorities, in *"consequence of some miscarriages at weddings"* which had occurred at the ordinaries, created a law prohibiting dancing in taverns on such occasions.

1633 Robert Coles fined for and made to stand with a sheet of paper containing the words DRUNKARD on his back for "*abusing himself shamefully with drink*".

1633 Under the guise of protecting quality, the Massachusetts authorities involved itself in the production of brewing, mandating a brew permit. William Whyte was accused of selling ale in this year without a permit, admitting he only wanted "*to brew a liitle beere, for ye Collyers and other workmen.*" The judges were not lenient on William, this was a time when colonial leaders were over concerned with the common practice of drinking at work.

1634 Samuel Cole is the first in Boston to be licensed to operate a tavern.

1634 Price of beer regulated at a penny a quart.

1634 Robert Coles (second appearance here) made to wear a red "D" on a white garment every day for one year.

1637 Robert Sedgewick made Captain for Charlestown and given license to brew beer for the Colony of the Massachusetts Bay (the first license issued to brew in America).

1637 Complaints arose of "*much drunkenness, waste of the good creatures of God, mispense of time, and other disorders*" at the ordinaries. Also laws were created regarding the sale of liquor to the "*devilish bloudy salvages*". Which no doubt referred to native Indians of whom several arrests, fines and punishments for liquor abuse were noted at this time.

1637 Illegal to sell *"cakes or buns"* in ordinaries except for those needed for weddings, funerals or similar events.

1642 In Boston "William Willoughby for being distempered with wine and misspending his time and neglecting both publique and private Ordinances was committed to Prison to be kept to worke there."

1643 Robert Wright was "fined twenty shillings for being twice distempered in drink or to sit an hour in the stocks the next Market Day in Boston."

1645 Landlords were restricted by the Court "to suffer anyone to be drunk or drink excessively, or continue tippling above the space of half an hour in any of their said houses under penalty of 5s, for every such offence suffered; and every person found drunk in the said houses or elsewhere shall forfeit 10s.; and for every excessive drinking he shall forfeit 3s. 4d.; for sitting idle and continuing drinking above half an hour, 2s. 6d.; and it is declared to be excessive drinking of wine when above." Although examples are rare, women were also punished severely for "intemperate drinking from one ordinary to another".

1645 Laws first introduced to curb the widespread practice of drinking at work. Having virtually no impact, a ration of ale was part of work contracts until well into the 1700's.

1647 Fines introduced for playing shuffleboard in taverns.

1648 By now the colony had "*hoalsome laws provided and published*" to encourage temperance. These were mostly ineffective.

1650 Bowling added to the list of banned tavern amusements. Incurring a fine of 20 shillings for the tavern owner and 5 shillings per player.

1651 The courts specified exactly what quantity of "*good barley mault*" should go into the brewing of ale to ensure taverns served good quality beer.

1656 General Court of Massachusetts made towns liable to a fine for not sustaining an ordinary. The reason being to facilitate local trade; by making the stay of Puritan businessmen more pleasurable, and therefore more frequent.

1656 Massachusetts church leaders successful in establishing a law making the sale or consumption of alcohol illegal on Sabbath.

1662 The "*tithing-man*", a tavern spy, is officially appointed to keep a check on consumption and gaming in the early ordinaries He inspected the houses, logged complaints and passed to the local constable the names of "*idle drinkers and gamers*". He cautioned landlords not to sell liquor to any whom he caught tippling too heavily. An English visitor in Boston, John Josselyn, in 1663, complained: "*At houses of entertainment into which a stranger went, he was presently followed by one appointed to that office, who would thrust himself into the company uninvited, and if he called for more drink than the officer thought in his judgment he could soberly bear away, he would presently countermand it, and appoint the proportion, beyond which he could not get one drop.*"

1664 Laws introduced prohibiting "singing rudely, or making a noise...in any place of public entertainment". The fine was 5 shillings.

1667 The issue of beer quality reached the Massachusetts courts. Regulations stipulated that beer had to be made from good quality malt, not diluted with sugar or molasses.

1698 Tavern keeper Edward Durrant arrested for allowing ninepins to be played in the yard of his tavern.

1701 Persons annually licensed in Boston to keep taverns and sell beer shall not exceed 6 wine taverns, 10 tavern keepers and 8 retailers of wine and strong liquors out of doors. The above provision did not keep up with demand and the county court licensed another 6 taverns in the same year.

1705 All new tavern licenses only granted to those of good repute, with convenient houses and at least 2 beds to entertain strangers and ability to provide 'pennyworths' (fixed price beer). The approbation of the Treasurer must be secured.

1710 Sheriffs and deputies given the power, when a tavern owner had his license revoked for an irregularity, to "*cause his sign to be taken down.*"

1711 Boston incurs a shortage of malt, so forbids the exportation of barley in panic.

1711 "No singing, Fidling, Piping or any Musick, Dancing, or Revelling shall be suffered" in a tavern.

1712 Sale of rum forbidden in taverns.

1756 Licensed Boston taverns reach 156 in operation.

1789 Massachusetts passes an Act encouraging the manufacture and consumption of beer and ale.

Although there was a lot of legislation surrounding taverns it must be put into perspective. The Pilgrim Fathers were certainly not known for their partying, extravagance or immorality so they naturally disliked taverns and their culture. However, even with their stern beliefs, tobacco was looked on as far more sinful, degrading and harmful than liquor. Lawmakers were not prudes either, they understood the need to keep people happy and healthy through beer, they even specified the amount of malt it should contain. But they too feared the effects of over indulgence. After 1720 the assembly enacted far fewer laws governing taverns in Boston. This may be due to the fact they had enough laws already, but more likely because they became increasingly aware of the impact these laws had on their constituents, who frequented the taverns. Restricting their constituent's pleasure, mostly at the request of the church, did little for their public image. Coupled with the fact that taverns had become big business and tavern laws were affecting some very powerful local businessmen, it became increasingly difficult to pass new legislation.

If all the tavern laws described above were actively enforced and obeyed, the Boston tavern scene would have been very quiet indeed. It was not. It is a fact these laws were neither enforced nor obeyed. A general disregard of statutes to limit alcohol consumption persisted during the 17th and 18th centuries. Beer was just too important to be pried away from the life of settlers and merchants in the new colony. The natural laws of supply and demand had more impact on ale consumption than any of the colonial laws ever did.

Ironically, as taverns increasingly became the subject of laws, they also became more crucial in exercising justice. Only a small budget for public works existed, so government buildings were non-existent in the colony's earlier days. Taverns became critical in helping to practice English law and therefore maintain order throughout the new colony. Traveling jurists moved from town to town presiding over cases. This became known as "*riding the circuit*". The jurists required use of a building in the center of the community, available for a minimal charge. Court was frequently held in the local tavern. There is no doubt that some of the most important decisions in the establishment of Boston in the 1600's were debated and decided in local taverns. John Turner hosted so many sessions of the Boston court in his tavern in the 1680's that he dedicated one of the rooms as court chambers. No doubt the lawyers would celebrate their wins in the taproom beside.

One famous judge who rode the circuit was Judge Sewall. The judge enjoyed beer and kept a malt house, but he did not patronize Boston's taverns for pleasure. Sewall could often be found presiding over cases in George Monck's tavern. One law he passed was very unpopular with tavern clientele. Created in response to Governor John Winthrop's observation that the drinking of toasts (including toasts to the health of him and his family as governor at the time) were getting out of hand in their number. John Winthrop wrote "*The Governor, upon consideration of the inconveniences which had grown in England by drinking one to another, restrained it at his own table, and wished others to do the like.*" The subsequent

1712 Act Against Intemperance, Immorality and Prophaneness, and for Reformation of Manners, was generally disregarded until Judge Sewall decided to enforce it on February 6, 1714. A bitterly cold evening, the shops had long closed and shuttered their windows, the streets were empty. In John Wallis's tavern a group had arrived to celebrate the Queen's birthday and had just begun their commemoration with a toast, then another, and another. A constable soon appeared at Judge Sewall's doorstep, dragging him away from the comfort of his fire due to a violation of the colonies latest law governing toasts. The justice of the Supreme Court and member of the Governor's Council walked into the taproom. He was greeted by everyone hoisting their mugs to the Queen's health and then a toast to his! Sewall was visibly unimpressed; the group had successfully infuriated him. The judge demanded their immediate dispersal and an hour of heated debate ensued. The revelers finally left and Sewall returned to his bed. The party regrouped at a nearby home of one of their members, to refuel no doubt, then marched to the Judge's house. Sewall was yet again dragged out of bed by the noise outside and threatened to call the militia. Leaning out of his window the judge demanded to know the names of the people gathered outside. One by one the crowd defiantly took it in turns to spell out their names at the top of their voice, believing the offence was too petty to warrant an appearance in court. However, Sewall later ensured they all got their day in court.

While on one hand the government encouraged the growth of taverns to facilitate trade, on the other hand they enacted laws, such as the one prohibiting toasts, no doubt to discourage the expanding political gatherings. Increasingly, the British Crown's authority was discussed at tavern gatherings, which concerned the Royal Governors. Another reason for controlling the number of taverns, according to David Conroy's book "In Public Houses", was to help the poor. The granting of a Boston tavern license could be likened to winning the lottery for poor people who, because of age, education or injury were unable to perform other forms of lucrative work, which involved trained skills or physical labor. As Boston became more commercialized and shops could easily be converted into taverns, the typical profile of a licensee shifted from wealthy businessmen to less fortunate people in society. Two groups of needy individuals that Boston selectmen felt particularly charitable to were widows and retired veterans. When the economy was doing badly, the local authorities were swamped with petitions containing details of people unable to escape debt. In order to obtain a license, these petitions included guarantees from friends that they were good citizens, with good intent to uphold tavern laws. Being granted a license was no guarantee of financial relief, however. The success rate of businesses with newly granted licensees was very low indeed. Such a high rate of failure was due to the large amount of competition from other liquor vendors in town and the high rents required for prime locations such as King (now State) Street.

Selectmen ultimately ruled over who could operate taverns. The number of license applications granted, rejected, re-applied for and removed altogether went up and down like a yo-yo throughout the 16th and 17th century as local governors came under pressure from various groups at different times. Such as existing tavern owners who wanted to restrict the number of new licenses granted to preserve their profits, the church, and poor individuals (essentially charity cases), who would become less of a strain on the community if they were given licenses.

Beer & Books

Before helping to establish Harvard College in 1636, John Harvard allegedly learned the art of brewing from William Shakespeare. Harvard made beer supply one of his earliest priorities by developing plans to construct a brew-house to supply both faculty and students. In contrast, the first President of Harvard, Nathaniel Eaton, ignored his responsibilities to supply beer, handing over control of brewing to his wife. She paid little attention to maintaining the beer supply. Rations were often nonexistent and by 1639 the students nearly revolted, complaining "*they often had to go without their beer and bread*". Lack of beer clearly contributed to Eaton's subsequent dismissal.

By 1667 beer was such a staple at Harvard that college rules governed operation of the college brewery in terms of the quality of both small and strong beer. In 1686 when Increase Mather, the father of Cotton Mather, was appointed to run the college, he drafted a Code of College Laws specifically for beer supply. Clearly specifying "*...each barrel consisting of sixteen gallons of Beer measure allowing thereto two pecks of Barley Malt*" to ensure both quantity and quality. Personal encouragement for brewing was also provided by Increase Mather. He wrote to the court on behalf of Sister Bradish, that she might be "*encouraged and countenanced*" in her bread baking, brewing and retailing of pennyworths—fixed price beer. His testimony states "*such is her art, way, and skill that shee doth vend such comfortable pennyworths for the relief of all that send unto her as elsewhere they can seldom meet with.*" Apparently students were allowed to buy a certain amount of beer. Considering the poor quality of their early housing, students needed as many pennyworths as they could get.

In its heyday of brewing Harvard boasted three fully functioning brew houses on campus. Beer was not the only drink available, during the Commencement dinner at Harvard in 1703, four barrels of beer and eighteen gallons of wine were served with one barrel of cider. Brewing beer gradually became less of a priority for Harvard, by the late 1700's the last brewery was relegated to a storehouse. The legend of John Harvard and his brewing skills is kept alive today at John Harvard's Brew House in Harvard Square.

ANATOMY OF A TAVERN

COLONIAL taverns were very different to the taverns of today in Boston. This section of the book reconstructs a typical tavern to help readers understand what a visit to a colonial tavern was really like. First; exploring the exterior, taking a look at tavern signs and names, then; stepping inside, describing the main rooms, equipment used to mix drinks, barkeep and entertainment available. The tradition of toasting is explained along with the terminology once required to order drinks and now long forgotten. The section appropriately finishes as most tavern experiences still do today: with the bill.

Signs & Names

If you were looking for an ordinary in 1600's Boston an "*ale stick*" or ale stake would be your best clue. A pole with a bush of barley tied to the top indicated what lay in barrels inside the otherwise residential looking building. Barley was the universal sign for beer. Tavern keepers also hung hoops of weaved barley outside their alehouse. Most people were illiterate in Boston at that time, but would recognize these signs. The tradition remains, bushels of barley are still used on bottle labels and other beer marketing today. The "*ale bench*" was another good indicator that you had arrived at a tavern. Weather permitting, the tavern keeper could be found outside, sitting on the bench with his patrons and maybe the local brewer. Ordinaries, which evolved from private houses, were originally known by the owner's last name. A good example of this is Boston's first ordinary, opened by Samuel Cole in 1633 and called "Cole's."

Over time, more effort was put into tavern signage. The first signs were carved in wood, stone or terracotta. Hung on wooden posts and wooden arms projecting from the tavern, or a nearby tree. The signs often represented hops or barley. More elaborate examples were made of metal, painted on tiles or included the head of a stuffed animal. Animals, particularly horses, could be found on many tavern signs in the 1700's. Hanging a picture of a horse outside a tavern would indicate that lodging with stables was available. This explains why so many establishments in New England were known as the 'Black Horse' from the simple sign they displayed. In fact there was a Black Horse, White Horse and a Red Horse tavern in Boston. Likewise, signs containing a horse and rider informed passers by that "*both man and beast are welcome.*"

Tavern signs were often borrowed from famous inns in Britain. This practice was good marketing; the tavern sign would appeal to passers by who had fond memories of their homeland. Examples include the Globe, St. George, King's and Queen's Heads, and Red Lion. Benjamin West was one of America's first well-known artists. He gained recognition for painting tavern signs for numerous inns all over the East Coast, no doubt in return for food, lodging and enough money to get him to his next assignment.

Up until the time most people could read, taverns were known simply by the image displayed on their signs, for example "at the sign of the Dog and Pot" would have been used to describe this location. The words Dog or Pot never appeared on the sign itself. Many of Boston taverns relied on business from the shipping industry, reflected in their nautical signs, including the signs of the Blue Anchor, Dolphin, Light House, Schooner in Distress, Ship, Noah's Ark and Admiral Vernon. 'Three' was a popular number; there were signs containing Three Cranes, Three Doves, Three Horseshoes and Three Mariners. By the mid-late 1700's, as literacy levels increased, words were placed on tavern signs. For example a tavern that relied on business from sailors may display the following couplet *"Coil up your ropes and anchor here, Till better weather doth appear."*

Taprooms & Tools of the Trade

Every tavern had one main public room, called the "*taproom*" or great room. William Black of Massachusetts described a tavern as a room with few tables, many chairs, and a happy, talkative clientele in "*Pleasures of Conversation and a Cheerful Glass.*" The taproom was normally low studded with great beams running overhead and hard white oak sanded floors. Taking up one side of the room, surrounded by chairs and tables for dining, would be the fireplace. Filled with huge blazing logs, cracking and sending sparks up the chimneystack into the crisp winter air. The smoldering embers competed with clay pipes inside the taproom to fill the air with smoke. In summer the fireplace would be decorated with green shrubs or neatly piled logs on firedogs or andirons.

On one side of the room, rows of untapped barrels containing New England rum, hard cider and beer were proudly displayed. In one corner stood the waist high bar, behind which beer casks were "*tapped*" by the landlord for serving. Most Boston taverns had 3-4 different casks of beer available and a couple of casks of cider. The landlord would be stationed beside his liquor behind a caged counter, amongst cans, bottles, glasses, jars of whole spices and whole loaves of sugar. The narrow closet-size area had a Dutch door that doubled as a shelf, with a barred gate that slid down on top of it. The device separated the tavern keeper and his liquor from his patrons. When tempers flared over political issues, often fuelled by alcohol consumption, it may have been necessary for the tavern keeper to lower and lock the "*bars*" securing his stock. Explaining the origination of the word 'bar'. Boston taverns were not all rough and unruly, nor were they all genteel.

All the tavern's business was transacted at the bar; patrons would arrange to stay in a room, get a meal or hear the latest news here. The inventory of the Golden Ball in Boston in 1790 lists on the shelves of the bar: large and small china punch bowls, wine decanters and glasses, tumblers and case bottles. Also behind the bar were a sieve and lemon squeezer, Bible, Psalm, and Prayer books. The bar equipment is representative of most of that era. Mounted on the wall was an old Scottish Highland Sword, which may indicate the origin of the tavern keeper at the Golden Ball.

The taproom walls were decorated with framed engravings, portraits of English royalty (when they were in favor), news bulletins and maps. Long wooden tables and high-backed benches would run down one side of the room. Tavern keepers placed durability above comfort. Chairs (normally rush-bottomed or Windsors) were not upholstered, floors were uncovered and windows were bare. The King's Arms tavern, one of the biggest in Boston during 1651, had only four chairs amongst a large collection of benches on which guests shared their seats. By the 1680's chairs were more popular, it was common to find as many stools as chairs in taverns, even so there was not enough for everyone. From a social perspective, benches contributed to the friendly atmosphere of early taverns by promoting sharing and fellowship amongst strangers. In contrast, chairs (a relative luxury at the time) encouraged individual importance.

Many features of the modern tavern that we take for granted were non-existent, such as indoor plumbing, refrigerated cabinets, air-conditioning and central heating. Other features have been outlawed today; fire codes ensure that sawdust no longer covers the floors, fireplaces are not lit and electric candles replace real ones. Another key difference, is a whole range of once essential utensils that have disappeared from Boston taverns today:

"*Bar spoon*"—a long handled wooden spoon for mixing flip.

"*Beer-pots*"—pewter tankards. Glass was too expensive, and pewter had no off-flavors like leather, wood or clay.

"Clay pipes"—tavern keepers offered European made white kaolin pipes for rental with the purchase of tobacco.

"*Growler*"—metal pail with a lid for transporting beer home.

"*Loggerhead*" or "*flip iron*"—found in every New England tavern of the time. Constantly kept warm in the ashes of the fire, waiting to be heated by the hot coals, to 'burn up' a drink called flip. The loggerhead served two purposes, to heat the drink and caramelize the sugars. Lowell describes a typical flip making scene:

"Where dozed a fire of beechen logs that bred
Strange fancies in its embers golden-red,
And nursed the loggerhead, whose hissing dip,
Timed by wise instinct, creamed the bowl of flip."

This picture illustrates tools of the trade involved in making American flip, a loggerhead (poker), mixing jug and extra long spoons. Served in a pewter mug.

Figure 2: Flip Making Equipment

"*Muller*"—early cocktail shaker. A large earthen vessel, kept on the mantle by the fire in the taproom. Shaped like an extra large beer mug or pitcher. Used like a mixing bowl, for creating beer-based mixed drinks.

"*Mullet*"—used to heat beer for drinks called "*cups*". Funnel shaped, with the narrow end closed. Kept on the grate of the fireplace amongst the coals.

"*Punch bowl*"—typically held a quart of punch. Made of china or tin-glazed earthenware called delft.

"*Quart measure*"—normally made of bronze. Taverns were required by law to purchase standard sets of measures. The size of each was stamped on its handle, from a gallon to a nip.

"*Scantling*"—a cradle made of crossed timbers to hold a cask of beer.

Nailed to the wall at the back of the taproom was often a small box with a tiny opening, bearing the words "*To Insure Promptness.*" Guests were expected to leave money in here to be divided between the servants. If not, they were politely reminded where to find the "*T.I.P.*" box. Tipping has remained customary in bars and restaurants ever since.

Tavern Terminology & Toasts

The following is a guide to colonial drinking terminology: A mixed drink was called "*Brewage*" since brewed beer was used in most mixed drinks. An undesirable combination of liquor, such as beer and wine was called "*balderdash*". Most mixed drinks were consumed hot (hot drinks were considered to have healing properties), in such cases beer was heated on the coals of a fire in a tall stone jug called a "*God-forgive-me*". Before a long voyage people would ask for "*Scurvy grass ale*", infused with watercress to ward off the dreaded disease of the same name. Alcohol in general was perceived to have a restorative effect, earning it the name of a "*Pick-me-up*" (nowadays we know it as a lay-me-down). A drink that did not mix well with the previous one was called a "*rider*". Acceptable mixes of beer included "*Nuts-and-bolts*", "*Half-and-Half*" and "*Light-and-Mild*", however "*Old and mild*" contained "*broken beer*" (old), so would be avoided; likewise "*Old Trousers*" contained all the partially consumed beers left at the bar, mixed together and re-served. It was cheap but best avoided. So to ensure freshness people liked to see the beer being tapped from the "*wood*" (the cask). A "*Hamster* " was a beer left momentarily left out of sight and picked up by someone else. A beer was "*skunky*" in aroma if over exposed to sunlight (there were no skunks in England so it was referred to as "*catty*" there). Brown and green colored glass bottles prevented skunky beers. A "*small beer*" was not small at all, but weaker in alcohol than a "*strong beer.*" Strong beer also kept longer, the alcohol was a natural preservative.

"*Tippling*" (drinking slowly) was encouraged; to avoid being called a "*Tosspot*" or an *"ale knight"* (both terms for drunkards). Another good term for being drunk was getting hit by "*ale passion."* In which case a person may find themselves at "*loggerheads"* i.e. in a heated argument with fellow patrons fuelled by alcohol. When people needed the bathroom they would ask for the "*heads*"; a term used by sailors to refer to the net under the carved head on the bow of a ship which suspended sailors in mid air when they needed to go. Having a good "*carouse*" (drinking and merrymaking) was the aim of most tavern goers, the idea being to minimize the "*head space*" (the unused space at the top of your tankard), and reduce your "*heeltap*" (liquid left at the bottom of the tankard). A common expression was "*drunk as a pig*", a reference to how pigs, like humans, become intoxicated when they consume fermented grain; the pigs behaved aggressively, grunted loudly, made sexual advances, fought, vomited and slept—sounds familiar. The morning after people may have felt like they had been "*kicked by the brewer's horse";* referring to their pounding headache.

Raising a mug of foaming beer to someone's good health promoted good spirit amongst everyone gathered in the taproom. People would drink to each other's health, the King's, Queen's, royal offspring, governor, his spouse, and his children, right down to the royal stable hand. The customary raising and clinking of glasses was preceded with a loud "*Huzzah*!"—a precursor to today's "*Hurrah*!" The Liquor & the Law section of this book describes how toasting got out of control in Boston and was made illegal at one point in time. The following is a toast from John Trumbull (1756-1843), designed to ignite patriotic spirits:

"While Briskly to each patriot lip
Walks eager round the inspiring flip;
Delicious draught, whose pow'rs inherit
The quintessence of public spirit."

This is a more humorous toast from the same period (author unknown):

"Lift em high and drain em dry,
To the guy who ays my turn to buy."

Landlords

Two characteristics could be found in every successful Boston tavern keeper; cheerfulness and a good sense of humor, and for good reason, without which their customers would have gone elsewhere. The landlord dictated the atmosphere of their tavern. Brissot wrote in 1788 of taverns and the respectable nature of colonial landlords, compared to their untrustworthy English counterparts: *"You will not go into one without meeting neatness, decency, and dignity. The table is served by a maiden well-dressed and pretty; by a pleasant mother whose age has not effaced the agreeableness of her features; and by men who have that air of respectability which is inspired by the idea of equality, and are not ignoble and base like the greater part of our own tavern-keepers."*

Many years after Judge Sewall, another judge called John Adams was riding the circuit. Adams recorded his tavern experiences in his journal and described virtually every landlord he met as the "*most genteel*". His description of the proprietors of the Ipswich Inn are good example: "*Landlord and landlady are some of the grandest people alive, landlady is the great-granddaughter of Governor Endicott and has all the notions of high family that you find in the Winslows, Hutchinsons, Quincys, Saltonstalls, Chandlers, Otises, Learneds, and as you might find with more propriety in the Winthrops. As to landlord, he is as happy and as big, as proud, as conceited, as any nobleman in England, always calm and good-natured and lazy, but the contemplation of his farm and his sons, his house and pasture and cows, his sound judgment as he thinks, and his great holiness as well as that of his wife, keep him as erect in his thoughts as a noble or a prince.*"

Boston landlords were frequently ex-soldiers or people holding public office; as a selectman, road commissioner, tax assessor, tax collector, constable, or town moderator. John Adams noted that in taverns people drank heavily while "*plotting with the landlord to get him at the next town-meeting an election either for selectman or representative.*" Keeping a tavern required the same skills and business acumen as keeping a house. By 1714, Boston's population of 10,000 was served by a total of 34 tavern keepers (12 were women), 4 common victualers (1 was a woman), and 41 liquor retailers (17 were women), plus a handful of cider sellers. The extent and role of women in tavern keeping is an interesting topic in itself. Women often became tavern keepers by acquiring their departed husband's license, permitted by local selectman to help the family avoid poverty. Selling liquor was very lucrative for the effort; however, like many of their male counterparts, women frequently employed slaves to help run their business.

Brew Houses, Cellars & Parlors

The first modification to convert a building into a tavern was the addition of a brew house. Before commercial breweries were established in the 1700's, beer was brewed in these brew houses; a lean to, added to get the heat and fire hazard away from the kitchen. Brew houses are still visible on some colonial taverns and houses today as a lower roofline extending from the main structure.

The next stage in tavern architectural enhancements would involve designating a room of the tavern specifically for guests, the taproom, described previously. Underneath the wooden taproom floor was a full cellar. In summer, the ground provided insulation, keeping the temperature inside the cellar cool and constant, permitting longer storage of the taverns valuable stock. "*Cellar temperature*" is still used today to refer to the stable 50 degrees Fahrenheit of most cellars. In addition to beer and cider, perishable foods and preserved foods such as fruit and pickled meat, were stored in the cellar.

In addition to the taproom some taverns had a parlor, these rooms became popular in the latter half of 18th century. Only the best establishments had a parlor, separated from the taproom and used exclusively as a lounge for women travelers, or available for hire to some wealthy person. The room was not as lively as the taproom, but very pleasant in winter with an open fireplace, which made "*the old rude-furnished room burst flower-like into rosy bloom.*" In the summer, the fireplace was still of interest, as explained by this unknown poet:

"'Tis summer now; instead of blinking flames
Sweet-smelling ferns are hanging o'er the grate.
With curious eyes I pore
Upon the mantel-piece with precious wares,
Glazed Scripture prints in black lugubrious frames,
Filled with old Bible lore..."

The sleeping arrangements in taverns were not as intimate and private as they are today. Tavern keepers placed guest beds in all the public rooms described above. Even after separate rooms were established for travelers it was common practice to share the same room with others and sometimes the same bed! Regular bathing was not a common practice, nor was laundering sheets. Travelers recommended, "*Search first before you enter* [the bed]." Female travelers were rare but could expect the same circumstances.

Entertainment & Games

The simple act of drinking and smoking; swigging from pewter tankards while nursing clay pipes, was the main draw for most Boston tavern goers. Beyond that, tavern rules and regulations are a great source of information on what people did in taverns, or wanted to do if they could. The involvement of Boston magistrates is a good indicator that a lot of people were spending a lot of their time enjoying these activities. Boston magistrates forbid certain "*Sports of the Innyard*" including dicing, tally, bowls, billiards, carding, slidegroat, shuffleboard, quoits, loggets and ninepins. Bowling games were very popular and came in many varieties. "*Dadloms*" is a good example; the game involved a miniature set of skittles, small enough to play inside the tavern with a small ball known as the 'cheese'. These local tavern rules were taken from a sign dated 1765: *"No skulking loafers or flea bitten tramps. No paying the wenches. No dancing tankards on the table. No dogs allowed in the kitchen. No cockfighting. Flintlocks, cudgels, daggers and swords to be handed to the innkeeper for safe keeping."*

The Bill: "Mind your P's and Q's!"

A minimal number of staff took orders and served freshly pulled drinks. Staff kept a running total of each table's consumption using the tab system. The tavern owner would remind his staff, particularly during crowded and lively periods to "*mind your P's and Q's*". Tavern slang for 'don't forget to update the running tally of those Pints and Quarts'. In England the phrase has been adapted today to remind people to be more polite by using their "Please and thanQ yous'". To alert patrons of the important rule of paying as you go, tavern keepers politely erected signs such as:

"Within this hive we're all alive. With whisky sweet as honey;

If you are dry, step in and try, But don't forget your money."

A picture was placed in one taproom of a dead dog, under which was written: *"Died last night: Poor Trust, Who killed him? Bad Pay."*

Fortunately, many old tavern account-books and bills still exist today; a typical example follows. Note the distinction between men and women in this example, with "*weomen*" achieving a better rate than men:

"Mug New England Flip..... 9d.
Mug West India Flip..... 11d.
Lodging per night..... 3d.
Pot luck per meal..... 8d.
Boarding commons Men..... 4s. 8d.
Boarding commons Weomen...2s."

Records exist of a minister's ordination in New England in 1785, attended by eighty people in the morning, who consumed 30 bowls of punch before even going to the meeting. The 68 who stayed for dinner drank another 44 bowls of punch, 18 bottles of wine, 8 bowls of brandy, and a substantial amount of cherry rum.

The Price of Rum:

Rum was not expensive, Rev. Increase Mather, a Puritan parson, wrote in 1686: *"It is an unhappy thing that in later years a Kind of Drink called Rum has been common among us. They that are poor and wicked, too, can for a penny make themselves drunk."* The price of rum over time, compiled from several records, is shown here:

1673 6s. a gallon
1687 1s. 6d. a gallon
1692 2s. a gallon
1711 3s. 3d a gallon (currency was depreciating)
1757 2s. a gallon
1783 1s. a gallon.

In the early 1780's, molasses used to make rum was sold from the West Indies at 12d. a gallon. Although distilling equipment was not cheap, profit potential was great. Burke, 1750 stated: *"The quantity of spirits which they distill in Boston from the molasses which they import is as surprising as the cheapness at which they sell it, which is under two shillings a gallon; but they are more famous for the quantity and cheapness than for the excellency of their rum."* Rum distilleries were very prosperous in the mid 1700's. Bonner's 1769 map of Boston shows that many distilleries were located along Boston's wharves or in the Essex and South Street neighborhoods. The oldest, owned by the French family and operated by Henry Hill then Thomas Hill, was founded here in 1714. Child's, another large distillery, was on Essex Street. Other notable distilleries were Avery's and Haskin's, both located between Beach and Essex Streets. By 1794 only 18 of Boston's 27 distilleries were still in business and all were running at half capacity. The decline was due to the availability of cheaper sources shipped in from elsewhere and rum's increasingly bad reputation from being the preferred drink of the poor and local drunkards. The Prohibition was the final nail in the coffin for Boston's distilling industry.

Colonial Bartender's Guide

Bartenders were known as a "*tapsters*"; reflecting their role in tapping barrels, or as "*barkeeps*"; since they kept the bar in order. In terms of drinks, a Miss Russell describes some of the *"strong waters"* available near Boston in the late 1700's, in the Old Ordinary, Hingham: "*Metheglin, Calibogris, Canstantia, Kill-Devil, Rumbullion, Alicanti, Spiced Syder, Switchel, Mumbo and Ebulum.*" In making sense of these concoctions one needs to examine the basic ingredients first to discover where and how these drinks originated. New England had an abundance of apples, pears, labruscan grapes, honey, and grain; therefore cider, perry, local wines, mead, and beer dominated the drink selection. In addition, trading ships on their way to the new world would stop off at the islands of Madeira to load up on barrels containing the drink of the same name. Portuguese wine was fortified with brandy to preserve the liquor during its journey to America (and increase its strength). Ships from England would bring whisky, from France brandy and from the West Indies molasses for making rum. A Mr. Bruce in the early 18th century states that "*Madeira, Canary, Malaga, and Fayal wines were probably much more abundant in the Colony that in England at this time, and were drunk by classes which in the mother country were content with strong and small-beer.*"

The most popular drinks in colonial times were Ale, Rum and Cider. The most common mixed drinks were Flip, Punch and Sack. All are explained in detail next, with authentic recipes, using all natural ingredients. Beer was traditionally served in "*pints*" and still is in the UK. For reference, a pint is 20 ounces, a gill is half a cup or 4 ounces and a jigger is 1 ½ ounces. Many of the recipes given in this book are authentic so you will see a variety of all these measures used.

Ale

Early colonists were not enthusiastic water drinkers. Ale was considered a healthier beverage than water because natural water resources had been polluted in the mother country and were thought to be here too. To brew ale the thirsty settlers needed malt, from barley, which was not native to New Enland, so the early settlers resorted to importing the ingredients required for brewing from their homeland. The brewing process was the responsibility of the woman of the house, aptly called the "*alewife*," alongside baking bread. Very early brews were fermented at warm temperatures with a type of bread yeast. The result; a nut brown ale, slightly sweet and lightly carbonated, served from the barrel several days after fermentation was complete. This ale was an excellent source of nutrients such as B vitamins, minerals and enzymes. Such hearty ales sustained the pilgrims, fortifying them during the "*starvation times*" of their first winters.

Ale was the older drink, made from malt, water and spices; beer was made later with the addition of a relatively new preservative and flavoring: hops. Fortunately, wild hops were native to America and the pilgrims found them growing in nearby forests. Small beer, which had only a small quantity of alcohol (1%), but large quantities of lactic acid and beneficial enzymes, was traditionally consumed in the morning. The beer accompanied a heavy breakfast of fish or cold meat, eggs and bacon. Strong beers, due to their higher alcohol content, were acknowledged as providing "*comfort for the poor.*" Pregnant colonial women sometimes drank what's known as a powerhouse beer called "*groaning ale*" while in labor. Wines from France and Spain eventually found their way to America, but were beyond the means of most. Instead families harvested barley and hops, and constructed brew houses beside their homes. Early ingredients in colonial brew kettles grew to include corn, pumpkins, parsnips, and oats to substitute the barley crop that often failed in the harsh New England weather. New England taverns were renowned for their inventive Spruce, Birch and Sassafras beer, boiled with numerous roots and herbs (birch, spruce, sassafras bark, pumpkin and apple parings) and sweetened with molasses, maple syrup, or beet tops. This colonial lyrical talent provides an insight: *"Oh, we can make liquor to sweeten our lips. Of pumpkins, of parsnips, of walnut-tree chips."* Walnut chips were sometimes added to improve the drink's smell.

Spruce Beer

This recipe is one of the oldest early American recipes for brewing beer, taken from Amelia Simmons's *"The First American Cookbook"*:

Take four ounces of hops, let them boil half an hour in one gallon of water, strain the hop water then add sixteen gallons of warm water, two gallons of molasses, eight ounces of essence of spruce, dissolved in one quart of water, put it in a clean cask, then shake it well together, add half a pint of emptins (semi-liquid prepared yeast, see below), then let it stand and work one week, if very warm weather less time will do, when it is drawn off to bottle, add one spoonful molasses to every bottle.

Emptins: Take four ounces of hops and about three quarts of water, let it boil about fifteen minutes, then make a thickening as you do for starch, strain the liquor, when cold put a little emptins to work them, they will keep well cork'd in a bottle five or six weeks.

George Washington's Small Beer

This recipe was penned by George Washington himself and found in his personal papers at the New York Library: *"To Make Small Beer: Take a large siffer full of bran hops to your taste—Boil these 3 hours. Then strain out 30 gall n into a cooler put. In 3 gall n molasses while the beer is scalding hot or rather draw the molasses into the cooler. Strain the beer on it while boiling hot, let this stand till it is little more than blood warm. Then put in a quart of ye[a]st if the weather is very cold cover it over with a blank[et] let it work in the cask—Leave the bung open till it is almost done working—Bottle it that day week it was brewed."*

Jingle

This seasonal drink was popular at Christmas in the 1700's and is similar to another well-known drink called "*lambswool*". Roast the apples until the skins burst. Warm the ale, mix in the nutmeg, ginger and sugar. Then place in the apples just before serving, while still hot.

3 small apples
3 pints strong ale
2 tsp nutmeg
½ tsp ginger
1 tbsp brown sugar

The following recipes did not make the cut:

Whistle Belly Vengence

An unusual drink was popular in Salem, Massachusetts in colonial times. It was made from sour old homebrew (proving New Englanders' notorious thriftiness). The old beer was simmered in a kettle, sweetened with molasses, filled with crumbs of "*ryneinjun*" bread (for thickening), and consumed piping hot. Also known as "*whip-belly-vengeance*", probably due to its impact on your digestive system.

Flap Dragon

This was popular in the 1600's to mid 1700's. Colonists would float a number of highly flammable liquors on top of beer, possibly some raisins as well. Just before consumption the spirits were set on fire. The mixture was drunk in one go, apparently extinguishing the flame as it went down. Flap dragon was even played as a game.

Rum

Tales of travel by stagecoach in New England, or of pirates running rife in the high seas off Boston, would be incomplete without mentioning a very American stimulant—rum. Either due to its taste when mixed with lemons and limes in punch, or because of its ability to induce intoxication faster than ale, rum became one of the most desirable drinks in Boston. Even Paul Revere, during his famous ride, did not start his cry "*The English are coming!*" until he had stopped at a rum distillery for a quick tipple. The oldest American reference to rum can be found in the act of the General Court of Massachusetts in May, 1657, prohibiting strong liquors to be sold in certain circumstances "*whether knowne by the name of rumme, strong water, wine, brandy, etc., etc.*" Colonials drank close to 4 gallons of spirits per year, of which most was rum, which averaged 45% alcohol (90 proof). Some tavernkeepers, according to their inventories, sold nothing but rum to their clientele; earning their establishments the title of "*grog*" or "*dram*" shops. A dram was a standard measure of rum. Grog was rum diluted with water, a standard daily ration for British sailors. Grogshops were the rowdiest of taverns, typically near the docks and full of seamen.

Rum is derived from the Latin word 'saccharum', meaning sugar. However, up until the 1700's rum was known as *Barbadoes-liquor*, *Barbadoes-brandy* or *kill-devil*; referring to its reputation as "*hot, hellish and terrible*". People in New York called rum "*brandy-wine*". Indians called rum "*ocuby*", pronounced in Norridgewock as 'ah-coobee'. There are many drinks that sound like rum but do not contain a drop of the liquid: *Rumbowling, rum-barge, rumbooze rambooze* and *rumfustrian* are all drinks named after the gypsy adjective "*powerful*". *Rumfustian, rumbooze* and *rambooze* are old English university drinks, *Rumfustian* consists of strong beer (quart), white wine (bottle) or sherry, gin (half pint), egg yolks (12), orange peel, nutmeg, spices, and sugar.

The English gave rum to the Indians to soften them up in early trade negotiations. Indians had little experience in their society of coping with alcohol and its consequences, some quickly became addicted to consuming the liquor. Laws were subsequently introduced, restraining the sale of rum to the "*bloudy salvages*" and records exist of people being prosecuted for violating these regulations. Over in New York the Dutch were too busy drinking beer, gin and schnapps, to appreciate rum. In contrast, they disagreed with Massachusetts' prohibition of rum sales to Indians, stating; "*To prohibit all strong liquor to them seems very hard and very Turkish. Rum doth as little hurt as the Frenchman's Brandie, and in the whole is much more wholesome.*"

New Englanders required molasses to produce rum, leading to the so-called 'triangular trade', a vital part of 18th century economics. Sugar and molasses flowed from the West Indies, to Boston, where it was converted into rum and then shipped to Africa in exchange for slaves. The slaves were transported inhumanly to West Indies plantations and forced to produce the molasses which was shipped to New England…and so on. New England rum was also smuggled into Spain and France for gold. The gold was then used to pay for English goods.

Even after the end of slavery, Boston continued to import molasses in large quantities to produce rum. At one time Boston was awash in molasses: On the water side of Commercial Street, opposite Copp's Hill, stood in 1919 a 2.5 million gallon storage tank owned by United States Industrial Alcohol. Constructed with great curved steel sides and bottom plates set into a concrete base and pinned together with a stitching of rivets. It burst creating a 14,000-ton sticky spillage that destroyed most of what lay in its immediate path. The Great Molasses Flood of 1919 killed 21 and injured 150. The cleanup operation took months and the stains can still be seen inside basements today in the North End.

Punch was the most popular mixed rink containing rum. In fact it was so popular that in the 18th century that tavernkeepers reportedly substituted rum with brandy when making punch. Other rum mixers included *"black-strap"*; containing rum and molasses. Josiah Quincy hoped the recipe of this drink would be lost in time. He states, *"Of all the detestable American drinks on which our inventive genius has exercised itself, this black-strap was truly the most outrageous.*" Across Boston casks of black-strap stood in every tavern with a salted cod-fish hung beside, to somehow tempt thirsty patrons. If black-strap was not to your taste "*Calibogus*," or "*bogus*" (unsweetened rum and beer) was also available along with "*mimbo*", abbreviated to "*mim*" (made of rum, loaf-sugar and water). Toddy, Sling and Grog are the closest you can get to these early rum concoctions in bars today.

Grog

In an 8 oz mug place all the ingredients in order, garnishing with the twist of lemon peel and a dusting of nutmeg or cinnamon.

1 tbsp strained lemon juice

1 tsp sugar syrup
(2 parts water to 1 part sugar, cooked over low heat until clear, then boil 1min)
1 jigger of dark rum
very hot tea or water
lemon peel
ground nutmeg or cinnamon

Punch

Despite what some people believe, Punch is not derived from the verb of the same name that depicts the impact the drink often has. Punch actually originated in another English colony, India. The word comes from a Hindustani saying "*panch, five*" referring to its five ingredients: Tea, arrack, sugar, lemons and water. In 1757 a S.M. of Boston, sent Sir Harry Frankland a box of lemons with this note, which explains the origins of punch:

"You know from Eastern India came
The skill of making punch as did the name.
And as the name consists of letters five,
By five ingredients is it kept alive.
To purest water sugar must be joined,
With these the grateful acid is combined.
Some any sours they get contented use,
But men of taste do that from Tagus choose.
When now these three are mixed with care
Then added be of spirit a small share.
And that you may the drink quite perfect see,
Atop the musky nut must grated be."

Interestingly the "*spirits a small share*" of the Puritan's punch was not the norm in Boston's notoriously strong punch recipes. The order and quantity of liquor in Punch was a much-debated topic. A local Irish ecclesiastic of high office provided this advice: *"Shtop! Shtop! Ye are not commincin' right and in due ordher! Ye musthn't iver put your whiskey or rum foorst in your punch-bowl and thin add wather; for if ye do, ivery dhrop of wather ye put in is just cruel spoilin' of the punch; but—foorst—put some wather in the bowl—some, I say, since in conscience ye must—thin pour in the rum; and sure ye can aisily parcaive that ivery dhrop ye put in is afther makin' the punch betther and betther."*

The English invented a bowl specifically for punch drinking, called a Monteith. The rim was scalloped for the punch ladle, lemon strainer and tall glasses; which dangled on their sides, feet out. The ornamental rim normally separated from the bowl, being lifted off with the glasses, ladle and strainer so the punch could be brewed inside. An 18th century society dinner would not be complete without a bowl of punch being passed around the table. In taverns, double (2 quarts) and thribble (3 quarts) punch bowls could be ordered. Juices of lemons, oranges, limes, and pineapples were used in punch concoctions. A Boston fruit importer called J. Crosby placed an advertisement in the Salem Gazette during 1741: "*Extraordinary good and very fresh Orange juice which some of the very best Punch Tasters prefer to Lemmon, at one dollar a gallon. Also very good Lime Juice and Shrub to put into Punch at the Basket of Lemmons, J. Crosby, Lemmon Trader.*" Punches took the name of their producers, whether amateur or professional, of hosts, of bartenders, of stagecoach drivers, of their strange ingredients or of the subsequent romantic incidents. The following are some of the more popular recipes:

Colonial Punch

Mix the following in order over heat for 5 minutes, stirring the mixture until it foams:

10 tsp sugar
1 pint hot water
juice of 2 lemons and peel
2 gills Jamaican rum
1 gill brandy
½ gill porter or stout beer
dash of Arrack

Colonial Wassail

This drink originates from the old English custom of 'wassailing' for Christmas and New Year celebrations: A large punch bowl filled with a spiced drink was served and everyone gathered around what became known as the 'wassail bowl' to toast the season. Mix the burgundy, cranberry, sugar, water, lemon juice, and cinnamon in a large saucepan. Heat just until bubbling around edges, then reduce heat. Simmer, uncovered, for 10 minutes. Remove cinnamon with a slotted spoon. Stir in brandy. Ladle punch carefully into mugs; garnishing with lemon slices. Serves 12.

1 bottle dry red wine (Burgundy)
2 cups cranberry juice
1 cup of sugar
½ cup water

¼ cup lemon juice
Cinnamon (6 inch stick)
¼ cup brandy
12 lemon slices

Hot Spiced Punch

Freshly pressed cider is mixed with spices from the West Indies. You can make an alcoholic or non-alcoholic version depending on the cider you use. Bring the cider, lemon and cinnamon to a simmer on a medium heat. Place the cloves in cheesecloth and make a sachet. Simmer in the cider for 10 minutes. Discard the sachet and cinnamon, add the nutmeg, serve hot in mugs. Serves 9.

4 cups fresh apple cider
1 large lemon strained (1/4 cup of juice)
4 sticks cinnamon
1 teaspoon whole cloves (6)
½ teaspoon freshly grated nutmeg

In the 17th century, nutmeg was a very popular flavoring for mulled wine and other spiced drinks. Nutmeg importation to America was completely controlled by the Dutch. High society and fashionable ladies would carry whole nutmegs in their pockets. In taverns where nutmegs were not available or of poor quality, people would grate their own nutmeg to add to their spiced drinks. The dainty nutmeg holder was one of the prettiest trinkets of colonial times. Made of wrought silver or Battersea enamel, there was room just for one. The inside of the cover was pierced to form a grater.

Flip

STEPPING into a 1700's Boston tavern and asking for flip would set off a chain of events unheard of in any bar today. Flip was one of the most popular drinks of colonial times. After receiving an order for flip, with pride the barkeep would leave the comfort of his bar and stroll over to the hearth. A jug of beer, left on the brick floor to steam gently by the fire, would be shifted closer to the hard-wood embers. The barman would then thrust a loggerhead (see 'Tools of the Trade' section) into the heart of the fire. He returns to his bar, scooping a pre-prepared concoction of fresh eggs beaten into a froth, cream and brown sugar, already chilled to 'age' for 2 days, into a pewter mug or earthen pitcher. Most bars added spices to make a signature mix, the recipe of which was a much-guarded secret, for example nutmeg was replaced with local ingredients such as cinnamon, pumpkin and apple. A generous serving of rum was then added to the mix. The barkeep would bring the tankard to the fire, pour in the steaming hot beer, stir, then thrust in the glowing red loggerhead. The drink would hiss as it boiled and a thick frothy head would appear as the sugars inside caramelized, sending a sweet spicy smell around the tavern. Beating a fresh egg into the mixture at the last moment would froth the drink so much it foamed furiously out of the mug, giving this flip recipe the name of "*bellows-top*". Although flip created a mess on the brick fire surround and took a long time to make, it was well worth the effort.

Flip is mentioned as early as 1690 in New England. Every tavern bill of the eighteenth century appears to be punctuated with entries for flip. Flip was no doubt a big hit in colonial times, John Adams mentions people drinking "*drams of flip, carousing, and swearing*" (the results of alcohol consumption have changed little today). Eventually flip, of British origin, was more popular in New England than England. Flip was perceived as one of the healthiest substances that could pass through your lips. Beer was perceived as healthier than the easily fouled drinking water, so doctors frequently prescribed beer-based mixtures as remedies for a variety of illnesses. Warm beer, being much easier to digest, was considered even healthier; therefore flip seemed an ideal medication. The drink even smelt healthy due to its spiced aroma. Flip was also known as "*Flip-dog*" or "*Hottle*" and cider was occasionally substituted for beer. Flip glasses from the 19th century can still be found in New England antique stores—indicating our ancestors appetite for flip—look for large splendid glass tumblers without handles, holding three or four quarts. Under December in the New England Almanac of 1704 a reference to flip is found:

"The days are short, the weather's cold,
By tavern fires tales are told.
Some ask for dram when first come in,
Others with flip and bounce begin."

Basic Flip

Take a pewter mug or earthen pitcher (quart size) and fill two-thirds with the beer. Sweeten with one of the options given depending on what is available. Then flavor with rum. Lastly thrust in a red-hot loggerhead (poker) and stir. The sizzling iron will make the liquor foam and bubble. The result is a burnt and bitter taste, with an indescribable smell that made the drink so unique and much loved in its time.

1 small bottle strong, bitter beer
1 tsp brown sugar or molasses or dried pumpkin (to taste)
1 gill or dash of Jamaican rum

loggerhead for mixing

Brandy Flip

A modern flip recipe.
2 oz Brandy
1 whole Egg
1 tsp Sugar
1/2 oz Light Cream
1/8 tsp grated Nutmeg
In a shaker half-filled with ice cubes, combine the brandy, egg, sugar, and cream. Shake well. Strain into a sour glass and garnish with the nutmeg.

Cider

Colonials became frustrated that the English barley required for ale production did not grow well in New England. Supplies from England were unreliable and not cheap. War created shortages of imported barley and malt, occasionally beer was hard to find in Boston. At the same time apple trees, not native to America, were delivering bountiful harvests. The cold crisp climate was, and still is, ideal for growing apples and also for the production of hard cider, a process easier than brewing beer. The eccentric clergyman, William Blaxton, planted the first cultivated apple orchard in 1625 on Beacon Hill. William became famous for training and saddling a bull to distribute the apples amongst his neighbors. Within a few decades of the Puritans arrival, every farm in Massachusetts had an orchard for apple harvesting (and cider production). Orchards yielded far more apples than people could eat. The excess became hard cider. Their apple juice kept at room temperature for less than a week before natural fermentation occurred. The resulting hard cider was potent, averaging 10% alcohol.

Cider was an extremely popular drink with early Americans, consumed at every mealtime; at funerals, weddings, ordinations, vestry-meetings, church-raisings, any opportunity people had. Drank from *jugs*, *pints*, *pots* or *pitchers*. The day started with cider, old men would have a quart plus of hard cider with their breakfast. During the day laborers in the fields drank hard cider from large draughts, fortified with drams of New England rum. At Harvard, students drank cider in two-quart tankards at dinner. Gentile ladies drank hard cider, even infants at night in their mother's arms, would receive hot mulled cider. Clergymen, while denouncing 'harder spirits', would drink cider as a matter of course. President John Adams said, "*If the ancients drank wine as our people drink rum and cider, it is no wonder we hear of so many possessed with devils*" (ironically in the later part of his life John started every day with a tankard of hard cider with his breakfast). In one year alone, cider production in Massachusetts reached 2 kegs for every person in the state. For New Englanders, hard cider was more prevalent than apple pie.

A History of New England Cider

1630's Cider production was tedious. Apples were pounded in wooden mortars. The pomace left behind was pressed into baskets.

1640's Basic mills were created, a springboard and heavy maul pummeled apples in a hollowed out log.

1650's Cider-making presses first appeared. Apples went for six to eight shillings a bushel and cider was 1s. 8d. a gallon.

1670 Everyone could afford cider and supply more than matched demand; as John Josselyn, a 17th century writer mentions "*I have had at the tap-houses of Boston an ale-quart of cider spiced and sweetened with sugar for a groat.*"

1703 Cider replaced beer and appeared in most people's daily diets.

1721 One New England village pressed and fermented over 3,000 barrels of hard cider, more than enough for the 40 or so families.

1728 Judge Joseph Wilder in Lancaster, Massachusetts, made 616 barrels from his land alone.

1740 An English traveler in Boston, called Bennett stated that "*the generality of the people with their victuals*" drank cider, which was plentiful and good at three shillings a barrel. It took a large amount of cider to supply a family when all drank, and all drank freely. Ministers often stored up to forty barrels of cider for winter use.

A popular cider based mix was *Beverige*. The recipe varied but included cider and water with ginger and molasses flavoring. Until recent times *Beverige* was drank in the summer by New Englanders in the countryside. The drink was often frowned upon because it was much easier to make than ale. Another cider variant was *Cider-Royal.* This involved boiling down four barrels of cider into one barrel, quadrupling the alcohol content. The inspiration for this probably came from making maple syrup. Cider diluted with water and called 'small cider' escaped much of the stigma of the early nineteenth century temperance movement but that did not prevent entire apple orchards being felled in the name of anti-alcohol morality.

When it came to hard liquor like rum, which required distillation and plumbing equipment, this was normally left to commercial distilleries. Applejack was the exception, made by freezing apple wine. A slushy ice forms on the top. A natural separation occurs between ice and the alcohol. By regularly removing the layer of ice, concentrated apple whiskey is left at the bottom. The alcohol content is increased well beyond the levels that fermentation can produce. Today, federal regulations effective since 1979 permit adult citizens to make as much hard cider as they wish. However, distilling cider to make hard liquor is illegal.

Switchel

Very similar to beverige but includes a dash of rum. Add the following ingredients in order and mix thoroughly.

2/3 glass hard cider
1/3 glass water
Jamaican rum (a dash to taste)

Gumption

Gumption is actually the general name for mixed cider and spirit drinks, of which "S*tonewall*" was one of the most potent. The following is an authentic 1790 recipe from Goodale Orchards, Ipswich, Massachusetts:

"While haying, or as a cool summer drink, mix 1 part black Jamaican rum with 2 parts slightly sweet hard cider and lots of ice."

Syllabub

Syllabubs were consumed either as a drink or as ice cream is today. They fall into three categories; the recipe for each is shown below.

juice of 1 lemon
2 ½ cups cider
½ cup brandy
¼ cup sugar
2 cups thick cream

Whipt. Chill a large bowl and put in all ingredients. Beat continuously, skimming off foam as it rises. Continue until all mixture has turned to foam. Put the foam in a serving bowl and chill in a refrigerator for 2 hours before serving.

Everlasting. A flavored cream pudding. If you want a dessert, a more solid version, whip the cream alone until it is stiff. Fold in the other ingredients and chill for an hour before serving.

From the Cow. This is the result of curdling warm milk being squirted directly from a cow into a bowl of cider. If you do not have access to a milking cow use preferably unhomogenized milk, otherwise combine homogenized milk with heavy cream. Heat milk to cow temperature (about 103 degrees) and use a soft squeezable bottle with a nipple to violently shoot the milk into the bowl, from about cow height. Chill for an hour then serve this drink immediately.

Other drinks from local fruits and berries included *Ebulum*: made from the juice of elder and juniper berries, with added spice and sweetening. Likewise *Perry* was made from pears, and *Peachy* from peaches. These drinks are still produced today in Southern England but are less popular on this side of the Atlantic.

Sack

SACK is a variety of the strong, dry, sweet, light-colored wines of the sherry family from Portugal and Spain. The price of Sack made it available to all classes by the late 1700's. Sack was most famously used in making a Sack-posset, drank at weddings by the bride and groom or at christenings. A famous recipe exists for Sack-posset, created by Sir Fleetwood Fletcher, appearing here from the New York Gazette, February 13, 1744 under the title "*A Receipt for all young Ladies that are going to be Married.*"

"From famed Barbadoes on the Western Main
Fetch sugar half a pound; fetch sack from Spain
A pint; and from the Eastern Indian Coast
Nutmeg, the glory of our Northern toast.
O'er flaming coals together let them heat
Till the all-conquering sack dissolves the sweet.
O'er such another fire set eggs, twice ten,
New born from crowing cock and speckled hen;
Stir them with steady hand, and conscience pricking
To see the untimely fate of twenty chicken.
From shining shelf take down your brazen skillet,
A quart of milk from gentle cow will fill it.
When boiled and cooked, put milk and sack to egg,
Unite them firmly like the triple League.
Then covered close, together let them dwell
Till Miss twice sings: You must not kiss and tell.
Each lad and lass snatch up their murdering spoon,
And fall on fiercely like a starved dragoon."

Governor Winthrop's first request to his wife back at home in England included the shipping of sack for the sailors. Still a century after landing at Boston, Sack-posset was a favorite at Puritan weddings. Judge Sewall describes one Boston wedding: "*There was a pretty deal of company present. Many young gentlemen and young gentlewomen. Mr. Noyes made a speech, said love was the sugar to sweeten every condition in the marriage state. After the Sack-Posset sang 45th Psalm from 8th verse to end.*"

Sack Posset

Yields 8 (1/2 cup) portions. Thoroughly blend all the ingredients except the sherry until well mixed. Pour into a saucepan and cook over medium heat, stirring constantly, until slightly thickened. Add sherry slowly, stirring constantly. Serve warm in mugs or chill before serving.

3 cups milk
1/2 cup granulated sugar
1 tablespoon flour
1/2 teaspoon nutmeg
2 eggs
1/2 cup sherry

Recreating a Bill of Fare

TASTELESS, bland and limited in choice are common perceptions of colonial food, however visitors to Boston taverns in the 17th and 18th century would have certainly not left with that impression. Patrons could expect wild game and fresh fish with seasonal fruits and vegetables gathered from around Massachusetts. Initially, Puritans adopted and adapted local recipes rich with native ingredients, including corn, artichokes, sweet potatoes, squash and beans, many of which were unavailable in Europe during the 1600's. The local area was abundant in wild foods such as fruits, berries, honey, game, wildfowl and maple. The sea also supplied a plentiful bounty of foods; low lying tidal areas around Boston hosted some of the richest oyster and clam beds on the East coast, farmed by Indians for centuries. In fact, lobster was in such abundance in the 1700's they used it as fish bait. Inland, early colonial farmers cultivated grains, flour, pigs and chickens.

Adapting recipes, often from Indians, early colonials created what have become very American dishes; Popcorn, Pompkin Pudding, Crookneck/Winter Squash, Indian Pudding, Hoe Cake, Johnny Cake, Molasses Gingerbread, Indian Slapjack, and Cranberry Sauce. To this day many of these recipes have not crossed the Atlantic with the same enthusiasm and so remain exclusively American dishes. An early colonial dish that has grown to epitomize traditional New England cooking is the one-pot meal. Examples include Boston beans, chowders, pot roast, casseroles and stews. These comforting meals were originally prepared in an iron pot large enough to feed the family and tavern guests for subsequent days. Based on Puritan ethics and thriftiness, such hearty 'no frills' dinners were referred to as "made" dishes; they saved on fuel (the pot was left to simmer slowly on the back of a wood stove), they made tough meat tender, and they freed up time for the cook to complete other tasks.

During construction of Boston's central road artery, named the Big Dig, archaeologists unearthed the remnants of one of the area's first taverns; The Three Cranes tavern in Charlestown. During the excavation they concluded that Bostonians ate a far higher proportion of meat pies than any of the other colonies. Meat pies were another type of made dish; Steak & Kidney pie and Shepherd's pie recipes were exported from England and proved just as popular in early America. Pies enabled leftover meat in the tavern kitchen to be safely re-used, despite having no refrigeration; cooking meat a second time eliminated any bacteria that may have developed since the meat was first roasted. Early settlers adapted their English pie recipes for locally found ingredients to create a new array of American pies including pumpkin, oyster, clam, spiced cranberry and grape varieties.

As Boston's shipping industry grew, a diverse mix of ethnic groups settled in Boston, each with their unique culinary style. Over time, Boston cuisine became a gastronomical melting pot, resulting in rich seafood chowders, smoked meats, homemade preserves and fruited desserts. The British introduced meat pies, along with hearty stews, scones and breads. The Germans bought sausages, soups and cakes. Africa and West Indian slaves bought their knowledge of curries, exotic spices and hot peppers. Hence, tavern cooks offered Bostonians a diverse assortment of dishes and the shipping industry supplied the diverse array of ingredients required to make them: Ships would carry Madeira; from the island of the same name, as ballast, from Seville—oranges, from Portugal—port, from the Spice Islands—spices, from Germany—gingerbread and cherries, from Jamaica—rum, mangoes and pineapples. Immediately after docking in Boston, Captains would auction goods beside their ships to tavern keepers eagerly waiting on the docks. Local produce arrived at the tavern up to three times a day; bread and pastries were baked fresh every morning, and with no freezer technology, meats were delivered daily. In general, food was far fresher than the produce served in taverns today.

People of all social backgrounds would feast in the tavern. One exception being that it was considered scandalous for a woman to eat alone until at least 1890. These common eateries had no menus, once inside patrons ate what they were given on long wooden tables filled with plates and soup bowls. In general, people ate dinner in taverns at a considerably earlier time than today; the main meal was served around 4pm. They shared food, family style:—eating in a tavern was an experience to be shared with others, not just a meal to satisfy oneself. Patrons took meat and poultry from large wooden platters called 'trenchers' while swigging on local brews from stoneware or pewter tankards. In the 17th century the food platters and the dinner table were not the only items that people shared with their fellow guests; tankards and large pots of posset were passed around the table amongst complete strangers. It was not until the 18th century that tavern owners gave their guests individual plates, cups, bowls and even forks. At first, ceramics were not very ornate and there were not many of them. However, by the late 1700's Boston tavernkeepers were providing their clients with fine exotic ceramics and beautifully blown wine glasses imported from the many destinations visited by the ships in the harbor. Imported tea was served in both European and Chinese tea wares.

Dinner normally had two courses, a first and a second plate. Dishes were spread upon the table for guests to take small portions; up to 20 dishes could have been served in one sitting. A typical feast would include two tureens of soup (for each end of the table), two fish dishes, mutton, ham, pork or beef, chicken or turkey and wild game such as pheasant or hare, served alongside boiled vegetables, sauces and relishes; such as jellies, salads, preserves and pickled foods. Early American cooking emphasized meat; wild game and fowl had the highest status, while white meats, fish and dairy products were less desired fare. Animals were grass fed, organically, producing free-range meat with its characteristic tough texture and strong flavor. Cuts were typically not as tender as today's so meat preparation took longer, involving long marinating periods, often 24 hours, and a variety of slow cooking methods. Chicken was served only on special occasions, as the hens were needed for laying eggs. Herbs and sallets (vegetable dishes) complimented the meats. Sweet dishes like dessert pies and custards were eaten alongside the first and second plates, not afterwards (waiting for dessert is a relatively modern creation).

In the best taverns, catering to the wealthy, a 'banquet' course was served after the first and second plates. The tablecloth was removed and replaced with fruit pies, cheese and wine or Madeira. Apples, pears, quinces and berries were stewed to make tarts, pies, pastries and puddings. All fruits and vegetables were thoroughly cooked because Europeans believed raw fruits were 'unwholesome'; medical books of the time cautioned against fresh fruits, which "*filled the body with crude and waterish humours, that dispose the blood unto putrefaction*" (Introduction to The English Housewife by Best). It could take 3-4 hours to get through a large feast. As glutinous as this sounds, the size of meat portions were a lot smaller than today. Even so, before the revolution an abundance of food was already considered an American birthright. Visiting Europeans were amazed at the appetites of colonials and how well fed they had become.

The sample tavern menu suggested here is derived from a variety of sources including Hannah Glasse's *"The Art of Cooking Made Plain & Easy"* from 1745 and Amelia Simmons's "*The First American Cookbook*" from 1796. In fact many of the dishes are much older. Research by the Plimoth Plantation museum suggests that similar recipes for roast fowl, cod, pompions, artichokes, frumentry, sallet, cheate bread and prune tart were served at the first ever Thanksgiving dinner. The following dishes are gradually disappearing from menus in America, so producing these meals for friends and family will help keep Boston's gastronomic heritage alive—bon appetite!

First Plates

Johnny Cake

Native Americans showed the Pilgrims how to cook with corn (maize) and most likely taught them how to make Johnnycakes. The original Johnnycake was a dry flat bread made with corn meal, salt and water, and baked on hot stones. The origin of the name is in dispute, possibly a corruption of Shawnee cake (from the Shawnee Indians) or 'journey cake' because it was easily prepared by travelers, or possibly based on some long forgotten Indian word by way of 'jonakin' or 'jonikin.'

1 cup cornmeal
4 cups water
1 ½ cups whole wheat flour
1 tsp. salt

Place the cornmeal and water in a pot, and bring to a boil. Lower the heat to a simmer and cook, stirring occasionally, until very thick (1/2 hour.) Preheat the oven to 357°. Blend the whole wheat flour and salt into the cooked cornmeal until well mixed. Place 1/2 cup size mounds, shaped like biscuits, on an ungreased cookie sheet and press down slightly. Bake for 15 minutes, turn cornbreads over (brown side up) and bake another ten minutes. Makes 2 ½ dozen.

Boiled Sallet

A sallet is a vegetable dish. Colonials boiled vegetables for up to an hour, believing raw vegetables were unhealthy, however they were boiling much of the goodness away.

1 firm, 2-lb. head of cabbage
1/2 cup currants
1/3 cup vinegar
2 oz. sweet butter
1 tbsp brown sugar

Separate the leaves of your cabbage, trimming away any shriveled outer leaves, then cut the heart into four pieces. Wash thoroughly. Fill a suitable sized pot a quarter of the way with water, adding ½ tsp of salt to every 3 cups of water. Bring the water to a boil. Plunge in your cabbage, cover with a lid and cook until tender. Remove form the heat and drain off liquid. While the cabbage is still in the pot, chop it well, then add the currants, sugar, butter and vinegar. Return to the heat and gently boil them together for five minutes. Serve in a dish, lay toasts of bread around the edge and sprinkle with a little more brown sugar, if desired.

Cheate Bread

Plan well in advance in order to make this heavy sourdough type bread. In a large bowl, dissolve the yeast in the warm water. Stir in the salt and flour. Cover and leave in a warm place for two to three days. The batter will bubble up, settle down and separate.

Bread:

2 cups warm water

2 tbsp dry yeast or 2 cakes fresh yeast

1 tbsp salt

2 cups whole-wheat flour

4 cups unbleached white flour

Soured dough starter

Dissolve the yeast in warm water. Add the salt and soured dough starter. Stirring continuously, add whole-wheat flour. Add enough white flour to make a soft, but not wet, dough. Turn onto a floured board and knead, adding as much white flour as needed to make a stiff dough. Knead for at least five to ten minutes. Return the bread to the bowl, cover with plastic wrap, and set in a warm place to rise. When doubled in bulk (1 1/2 to 2 hours), press down and turn onto work surface. Form into two round loaves or rolls, cover and place on cookie sheets that have been sprinkled with cornmeal. Cover and allow to almost double in bulk. Bake in a preheated 350° oven, scoring the loaves or rolls with a sharp knife just before they are placed in the oven. Bake for 20 to 40 minutes, depending on the size of the loaf. They are cooked when tapping on the bottom produces a hollow sound. Wrap the loaves in a dishtowel to cool. Serve with butter.

Clam Chowder

This is a traditional recipe for white clam chowder. Enough to serve 6, it's best with fresh clams. The Indians taught the pilgrims how to go quahogging—using your feet to find hard-shell clams called quahogs. You can try this technique today. Standing waist deep in a clam bed at low tide, repeatedly twist your body from side to side, drilling your feet into the sand. If you are lucky you will feel the edge of a clamshell on the bottom of your feet.

1 qt. soft shell steamed or chowder clams

3 small potatoes, peeled and diced

1 medium onion, finely chopped

3 slices bacon cut into small pieces
3 cups milk
1 cup heavy cream
1 tbsp butter
Salt
Freshly ground black pepper

If you have fresh clams scrub them thoroughly and soak them in three changes of cold water to remove all the sand. Steam clams over one cup of water for eight minutes until the shells open. Discard the shells and chop clams into small pieces. Strain the broth through cheesecloth to remove any sand. Boil the potatoes in salted water for 15 minutes. Fry the bacon in a saucepan until one tablespoon of fat has rendered. Remove the bacon. Fry the onion for three minutes in bacon fat. Add the strained clam broth. Simmer for five minutes. Add chopped clams, milk, cream, butter and potatoes. Season with salt and simmer for five minutes or until potatoes are just tender. Garnish bowls with a sprinkling of freshly ground pepper and reserved bacon.

Roasted Chestnuts

Chestnut trees once filled New England forests. Use plump fresh chestnuts, heavy for their size and free from blemishes and cracks. Refrigerate and use within 3-4 days. You can either cook them on the stove, in the oven, or on an open fire.

Oven roasting: Preheat oven to 400°. Cut an "X" in the round side of each nut to prevent them exploding. Cook for 15 to 20 minutes until tender.

Fire roasting: Cut as above and place nuts in a tin or pie dish with holes pierced in the bottom. Arrange nuts in a single layer and place on a grill above the hot embers. A more hazardous approach is to put them on the edge of an open fire and watch them pop.

On the stove: Cover the nuts with water and bring to boil for 10 minutes. Remove a few nuts at a time and cut them in half. Scoop out the meat with the tip of a teaspoon.

Roast Fowl

Goose, swan, or turkey, were frequently cooked in this manner.

1 10 lb. Fowl
1 cup oats
3 large onions
3/4 cup water

1/4 cup vinegar
2 tsp sage
2 tsp thyme
1 tsp marjoram
salt and pepper to taste

Parboil the oats in water until slightly soft. Then peel and slice onions. After straining the oats, mix them gently with the onions. Preheat oven to 325°F. Remove the giblets and neck from your fowl. Wash inside and out. Dry thoroughly. Stuff the body loosely with the cooked oats and onions. Place on a rack in a large roasting pan. Roast uncovered for 2 hours. Remove the fowl from the oven. Draw off the fat. Return to the oven and cook for 1 more hour.

Sauce: Take the drippings from the flow with some of the oats and onions. Mix well with the sage, thyme, marjoram, salt and pepper. Stir in the vinegar. Bring gently to a boil.

Place fowl on a serving dish. Drench with sauce and serve while hot.

Whole Cranberry Sauce

Sea captains were aware of the powers of cranberries in preventing scurvy, containing so much vitamin C that even after a year of storage they still delivered a nutritional punch. The color differences you find in cranberry skins is more to do with variety than of age.

2 cups water
2 cups sugar
4 cups cranberries
2 teaspoons grated orange rind

Place the water and sugar in a saucepan and stir until the sugar is dissolved. Boil the syrup for 5 minutes. Wash the cranberries thoroughly and pick out the bad ones. Simmer the cranberries in the syrup uncovered, without stirring. It takes about 5 minutes until they are thick and clear. Skim off excess. Stir in the orange. Pour the cranberries into a mold that has just been rinsed in cold water. Chill until firm.

Seethed Cod or Bass

1 3-4 lb. whole cod or bass
1 1/2 cup fresh water
1 tsp salt

Clean and gut the fish (or get your fishmonger to do this). Lay the fish in a pot and cover with just enough water. Add 1tsp. of salt. Bring very gently to just below boiling. Simmer for 10-15 minutes per pound of fish. Adjust for the thickness of your fish rather than its weight. When you can flake the flesh from the bone easily the fish is cooked. Do not overcook otherwise it will break into pieces. Putting the fish in cheesecloth before boiling can prevent this. Remove the fish from pot. Place fish on a platter while you mix the sauce.

Sauce:

¾ cup dark beer (or fish broth)

1/4 tsp dried rosemary

1 large onion, sliced

1/4 cup chopped fresh parsley

1/4 tsp pepper

1 tbsp Butter

Mix all the ingredients in a saucepan. Gently boil until flavors are well blended. Pour over your fish.

Steak & Kidney Pie

Pies were very popular in colonial times. You can make this without the kidneys if you wish.

1 pound lean stewing beef, trimmed and cubed

1 pound ox kidney, cored, chopped, washed and soaked in warm water

2 tbsp salt and freshly ground pepper

2 tbsp butter

1 tbsp oil

1 large onion, chopped

1 cup beef stock

Milk for brushing

Heat oil and butter together in pan. Toss the steak and kidney in seasoned flour, then fry in hot butter and oil until well browned. Put mixture on a plate. Add onion to remaining butter in the pan and fry gently until slightly golden. Add meat back to pan and pour in beef stock, slowly bringing to a boil. Lower heat, cover and simmer for 1 to 2 hours, stirring occasionally until meat is tender. Remove from heat; leave the mixture to stand until it is completely cold. Roll out half of the pastry on a floured surface, then use it to cover a lightly greased 9-inch pie plate. Trim away excess pastry. Roll out remaining pastry to make a lid. Pile on the cold meat with sufficient gravy in middle and moisten the edges of the pastry with water. Cover with the pastry lid, pushing edges together to seal, and flake by cutting with the back of a knife. Flute, then stand pie on a baking sheet. Brush with milk and bake in oven for 25 to 30 minutes, or until golden brown.

Pastry for a 9-inch double crust pie:

2 ½ cups all-purpose plain flour
½ tsp salt
½ cup chilled unsalted butter cut into small pieces
¼ solid vegetable shortening, chilled
1 tsp white vinegar
6-7 tbsp ice water

In a mixing bowl combine flour and salt. Add the butter and shortening and mix until the dough is crumbly. Pour in the vinegar and 6 tablespoons of water. Mix until the dough begins to come together, add more water if too dry. Put the dough on a clean work surface. Divide into two pieces, the bottom larger than the top crust. Flatten each into a thick disk. Wrap separately and refrigerate for at least 1 hour.

Boiled Jerusalem Artichokes

3 lbs. Jerusalem artichokes
1 tsp salt
4 tbsp butter

Thoroughly scrub the Jerusalem artichokes under running water. Place in a pot of boiling water. Cook until just tender, approximately 15 minutes. Drain, peel and mash with butter and salt.

Boston Beans

Boston gets its nickname "Beantown" from one of the Puritan's favorite dishes; Beans slow-baked in molasses. Cooking on the Sabbath was once prohibited, so beans were prepared on a Saturday, then baked overnight and still piping hot when served for dinner on Sunday. Originally made in a "bean-pot"—a stoneware vessel with a small top and bulging sides, designed to reduce evaporation and contain the heat well after the beans were cooked.

16 ounces (2 cups) dry navy beans
2 quarts cold water
1/2 tsp salt
1/2 cup molasses
1/3 cup brown sugar
1 tsp dry mustard
4 ounces salt pork
1 medium onion, chopped

Rinse beans and add to water in saucepan. Bring to boil and simmer for 2 minutes. Remove from heat, cover and let stand for 1 hour (or add beans to cold water and soak overnight). Add salt to beans and water, cover and simmer till beans are tender (about 1 hour). Drain, reserving liquid. Measure 2 cups liquid, adding water if needed, mix with molasses, brown sugar, and mustard. Cut salt pork in half and score one half. Grind or thinly slice remainder. In a 2-quart bean pot (or casserole pot), combine beans, onion and ground salt pork. Pour molasses mixture over. Top with scored pork. Cover and bake in oven at 300° for 5 to 7 hours. Add more liquid if needed. Makes 8 servings.

Standing Dish of Pompions

This is called a 'standing' or 'standard' dish because it was eaten everyday or even at every meal. Colonials called both pumpkins and squash 'pompions'. The dish needs plenty of time to cook and is served without a crust.

8 cups peeled diced pumpkin
2 tbsp vinegar
1/4 cup water
1/3 cup brown sugar
2 tbsp butter
1/4 tsp cinnamon
salt to taste

Put 2 of the 8 cups of pumpkin and 1/4 cup of water into a pot. Cook gently using a low heat until they sink to the bottom. Gradually add more pumpkin until you have used all 8 cups. The cooked pumpkin will be tender and have kept much of its form, like stewed apples. Do not add any more water. Remove from the heat and add the butter, vinegar, brown sugar and spices. Stir gently and serve.

Second Plates

Indian Pudding

Resourceful colonial cooks learned to make a wide variety of breads, puddings, and pies from cornmeal. Indians taught them how to bake this pudding with molasses as a sweetener, hence the name 'Indian Pudding'. This recipe serves six. It has become a New England tradition to serve Indian Pudding with vanilla ice cream.

2 tablespoons butter
3 cups milk
1/3 cup molasses
1/3 cup cornmeal

1 egg
1/4 cup sugar
1/2 teaspoon cinnamon
1/2 teaspoon ginger
1/4 teaspoon salt

Preheat oven to 300°. Grease the bottom and sides of a baking dish with 1 tablespoon of butter. In a saucepan, combine milk and molasses. Gradually stir in cornmeal. Cook and stir over medium heat until mixture thickens—about 10 minutes. Remove pudding from heat and stir in the other tablespoon of butter. In a small mixing bowl, beat the egg, add sugar, cinnamon, ginger, and salt. Gradually add egg mixture to hot cornmeal pudding. Pour the pudding into a greased baking dish. Bake, uncovered, for about 1 1/2 hours or until pudding has thickened.

Prune Tart

Pastry:
7-9" pie dish
3/4 cup wheat flour
1/4 cup all purpose flour
1/2 tsp salt
3/4 cup fat (butter or lard)
cold water to mix

Mix together the flour and salt. Rub the fat into the flour until it resembles fine breadcrumbs. Make a well in the center of your mixture and pour in enough cold water to bind the ingredients together; don't make it too sticky. Then mix thoroughly with your hands until it forms a stiff paste. Place onto a floured board and roll out to fit your pie dish. Ease your rolled pastry into the pie dish and trim the edges. Prick the bottom pie with a fork and cover with a waxed paper. Fill your pastry case with beans or rice and bake in a 400° oven for 1/2 hour. Remove the wax paper and beans and return the pastry case to the oven for five minutes to dry out the bottom of the pie case. Allow to cool.

Filling:
1 1/2 lbs. pitted prunes
1/2 cup fresh water
4 tbsp brown sugar
1 whole stick cinnamon
few sprigs dried or fresh rosemary
2 tbsp rose water

Mix together your prunes and fresh water, 2 tbsp sugar and whole cinnamon with a little of the rosemary, set the rest aside for garnishing your tart later. Bring all of the ingredients to a steady boil and cook for five to ten minutes. Remove from heat, discard cinnamon. Mash into a pulp and drain off excess liquid. Add remaining sugar and rosewater and stew again. Allow to cool, then fill up your pie case and garnish with sprigs of rosemary.

Frumenty

This dish contains hulled wheat cooked in milk and seasoned with spice, sugar etc. and tastes similar to creamed wheat.

1 cup cracked wheat
1/8 tsp ground mace
1 quart water
1/2 tsp ground cinnamon
3/4 cup milk
1/4 cup brown sugar
1/2 cup heavy cream
2 egg yolks
1/2 tsp salt
additional brown sugar for sprinkling

In a large pot, bring the water to a boil and add the wheat. Lower heat to simmer, cover and continue to cook for 1/2 hour, or until soft. Drain off all the water and add the milk, cream, salt, mace, cinnamon and sugar. Continue to simmer, stirring occasionally, until most of the liquid is absorbed (20 to 30 minutes.) In a small bowl, beat the egg yolks and slowly stir 1/2 cup of the wheat mixture into the yolks. Then stir the yolk mixture into the pot. Continue cooking for another five minutes, stirring frequently. Serve sprinkled with brown sugar.

OLD BOSTON TAVERNS UNEARTHED

Background

SAMUEL Adams, the patriot, is still seen around Boston taverns today. A simply dressed and originally austere man, his overly cheery smile appears on beer bottles, advertisements and beer pumps of bars supplied with Sam Adams beer by the Boston Beer company. Samuel (no one but his enemies called him "Sam") was a better brewer of dissent than of beer. Being a brewer it was his job to frequent the taverns of Boston, his clients, by day. And at night, along with his fellow rebel rousers; Joseph Warren (physician), James Otis (attorney), John Hancock (a young ship owner), Paul Revere (silversmith) and his cousin John Adams (lawyer), they could often be seen raising glasses to the demise of King George III's rule. This chapter charts the establishments that these men and others frequented and the events that occurred therein that make Boston taverns so rich in history. Boston taverns spanned the spectrum of the hospitality scale. At one end catering to the every whim of Boston's elite, and at the other end, providing rapid relief of every form to sailors as they first came ashore.

Two sources were particularly helpful in compiling this comprehensive list of Boston taverns over time: The work of Miss Thwing's on the "*Inhabitants and estates of the Town of Boston, 1630-1800*" from the early 1900's, based on *The Book of Possessions* and Town Records. Plus Samuel Adams Drake's "*Old Boston Taverns and Tavern Clubs*" from 1917. The many other sources consulted are referenced in the bibliography. The date shown beside each tavern represents the first recorded mention of the tavern, often due to the granting of a license. The location is listed, if known, of every tavern that existed from the 17th century to the start of the 19th century.

Finding the exact location of old taverns in Boston was not an easy task for several reasons: Streets went unnamed in early colonial Boston, throughways were described instead by the prominent buildings they once hosted. Many streets that were eventually named had their names changed over the last century; for example, several Boston streets were renamed after wealthy people of the time. Streets that were named and not renamed caught on fire; the great fires, of which there were eight between 1653 and 1711, further complicate the task of locating taverns. The fires destroyed many of the central taverns during some point of their lifetime. Tavern names also changed over time, making it difficult to fix their location; the main reason being that references to British rule such as King's Head, Cromwell's Head, British Coffee House and the Royal Exchange became unpopular with the locals. Despite these complications, the following list of early Boston taverns and their locations is believed to be the most comprehensive and inclusive compiled to date.

Taverns were so prominent in Boston during the 1600's that directions around town were often giving in terms of taverns, and their respective signs. Asking for directions in 1600's Boston, an early settler may have advised *"take a right at the Sign of the Blue Anchor and its three doors along from the Sign of the King's Head".* Taverns were often named after the elaborate signs they displayed outside, the Lion, Swan and Punch Bowl are great examples. As streets became named, sign-posts erected and houses numbered, tavern signs became less prominent. These individually unique signs that swung over sidewalks for decades, gradually disappeared over time. Some tavern signs lingered due to their humor, or as a guarantee of an established business, and some because people were just used to them being there. The only surviving signs that may exist today once hung outside the Bunch of Grapes and Hancock House. They were both noted in inventories of different local historical societies, but after extensive research can no longer be traced (if anybody knows where these signs are today please contact the author). The good news is that a handful of Boston streets are still named after the tavern signs they once hosted, namely; Black Horse Lane, Bull Lane, Cross Street, Orange Tree Lane, Red Lion Lane, and Sun Court.

By far the most important street throughout Boston's tavern history is King (later renamed State) Street. This road was the hub of commerce in Boston; the constant flow of business people made it an ideal location to operate a tavern. Only the most successful taverns thrived amongst competition from numerous other drink sellers, sometimes located just two doors away. However, by the mid 1700's, houses on King Street and the wharf at the end had become too expensive for tavern keepers to rent. Such is the laws of supply and demand that only Boston's super taverns, most notably the Bunch of Grapes, the Exchange and the British Coffee House, continued to operate profitably and survive comfortably on King Street. Even today State Street remains one of the most sought after locations for bar owners in Boston.

A-Z List of Boston Taverns 1630-1830

Anchor also **Blue Anchor, Fairbanks,** 1646, east side of Washington Street between State and Water streets. Richard Fairbanks, tavern keeper, had a house and garden here according to the *Book of Possessions.* The first overseas mail from Europe was received at Fairbank's tavern in Boston in 1639. The tavern was America's first post office. Letters were distributed by pinning them to one of the two main 'posts' that supported the entrance to the tavern's cellar. These hatchways were often constructed from sturdy wooden beams recycled from old ships. In fact some believe that's where the word "*Post*" originates from in America. Fairbanks, like most early American taverns, served as the local Post Office. These early post services were not very secure, the person who picked up the letter for delivery would often open it looking for the latest news. America's first purposely-designed Post Office was later built on the very same spot as Fairbank's tavern.

In 1686 John Dunton, a London author and bookseller visited Boston. He described George Monck, landlord of this tavern, then known as the Blue Anchor, from 1690-91: "*A person so remarkable that, had I not been acquainted with him, it would be a hard matter to make any New England man believe I had been in Boston; for there was no one house in all the town more noted, or where a man might meet with better accommodation. Besides, he was a brisk and jolly man, whose conversation was coveted by all his guests as the life and spirit of the company.*" Monck's tavern was also a popular place of work for the famous circuit judge, Sewall, who passed many a judgment while the General Court of Massachusetts was hosted in the Anchor. When Robert Turner kept the tavern he named rooms after old London inns such as the Cross Keys, Green Dragon, Anchor and Castle Chamber, Rose and Sun Low Room. The tavern's name undoubtedly originates from its sign, which probably displayed the Royal Navy insignia—an Anchor. The tavern was destroyed in the great fire of 1711. Now the site of the Globe building.

Baulston, 1637, West side of Washington St. between Dock Sq. & Court St. This is Boston's SECOND recorded ordinary. Owned and operated by William Baulston. Like many early houses of entertainment it was simply known by the owner's last name.

Bell in Hand, 1795, 45 Union St. Boston city's last town crier, "Old Jimmy" Wilson, after 50 years of announcing news, including the Boston Tea Party and the birth of a nation, decided to open a tavern. The Bell in Hand is one of Boston's oldest remaining taverns, but in name only. In 1795 Wilson opened the Bell (aptly named due to his previous bell ringing occupation) after purchasing Samuel Adams' house on Eliot Street (this location later became the Exchange Coffee House). In 1854 the sign of the Bell appeared in Pi Alley on Newspaper Row and thrived due to a bustling trade with printers, journalists, politicians and students. The tavern later moved to Devonshire Street and can now be found on Union Street. A close resemblance of its original sign swings over the heads of passers by today.

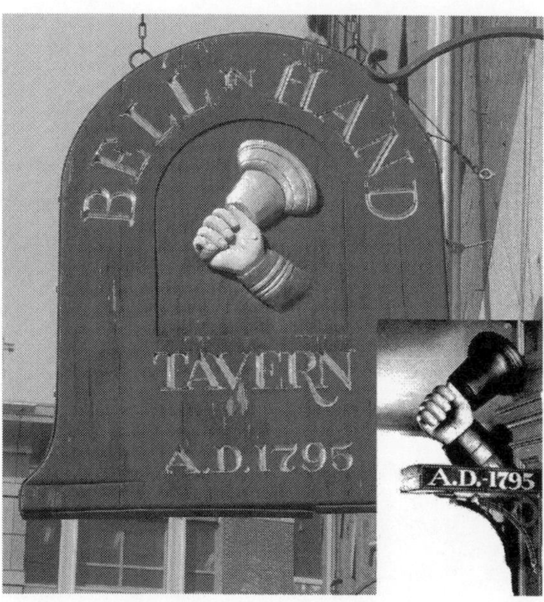

Figure 3: Bell in Hand sign—Then & Now—courtesy of The Bostonian Society

Bite, 1795, Faneuil Hall, west of Change Avenue. A favorite place for men who worked in the market at Faneuil Hall. James M. Stevens was its last landlord when it ceased to operate around 1860.

Black Horse, 1684, west side of Prince St. (once called Black Horse Lane). As was often the case the street took the name of its tavern. Mentioned as a hiding place for deserters from Burgoyne's army (British) when stationed nearby in Cambridge.

Black & White Horse, 1767, Robert Sylvester.

Blue Anchor, 1664, No. 254 Washington Street, also mentioned as being near Haver's Dock. Typical in location of Boston taverns, the Blue Anchor provided convenience for sailors on the waterfront. Thomas Bailey, landlord offered "*Refreshment & Entertainment of Boatmen and others*". Mentioned in 1760 "*land where the Blue Anchor was before the fire at Oliver's Dock.*"

Blue Anchor, (the second of that name) 1665, Brattle Street, on the same site that became **Doolittle's City Tavern**. Kept by Robert Turner, it was a favorite haunt of public men and noted for its punch.

Blue Anchor (the third of that name) 1735, northeast corner of Water and Batterymarch streets. Joseph Wilson was the landlord.

Blue Bell, West side of Union St. between Hanover and North streets. In 1663 John Button sells to Edmund Jacklin his house, known as Blue Bell.

Blue Bell, also **Blew Bell, Castle,** 1692 South West corner of Battery March and Water Street (Liberty Square). Kept by Nathaniel Bishop, then by Alleric & Drury. Known as the **Castle Tavern** in 1692. No longer used as a tavern in 1707.

Brazen Head, (east side of Washington streets between State and Water streets). Owned by widow Jackson. A soldier with smallpox is recoded here in 1757 and in 1760 the great fire broke out here.

Figure 4: Signs of the Baker's Arms, Dog n'Pot, Good Woman & Brazen Head

Brewer's Arms, east side of Washington between Bradford and Essex streets. Changed hands in 1696.

British Coffee House, 1762, also **American Coffee House** 1776, 66 State St. between Change Avenue and Merchant's Row. The coffeehouse concept was transplanted to Boston in 1678, 20 years after its appearance in London. In the 18th century tea was well established in the home, while coffee was enjoyed more in taverns. Managed by Cord Cordis, his wife Hannah, and two slaves, the British Coffee House was less ornate than the Crown Coffee House but much bigger and able to accommodate large companies of British Officers.

The first official 'club' in Boston was formed here in 1751, known as the Merchant's Club. Membership was restricted to merchants, crown officers, members of the bar, military officers and gentlemen of high society. The club offered the best of culture, wit and companionship for the powerful and elite. The first seeds of patriotism were sewn in this tavern when James Otis, John Adams, Cushing, Pitts, Dr. Warren and Molyneux met here to discuss politics. The tavern was popular with members of the bar, of which James Otis was a great legal mind and satirist. He was probably the most feared by the loyalists. When the political climate changed in Boston a number of patriots deserted what was becoming a tory sanctuary to form the Whig Club at the *Bunch of Grapes*. The British Coffee house was becoming a favorite hangout of loyalists and British Officers that accompanied the influx of British troops in 1768, becoming their unofficial HQ.

On September 5th the radical Otis, mentioned above, marched down King Street to the coffeehouse, enraged by letters written by British Customs Commissioners and leaked to the Sons of Liberty. After practicing his wit on customs officials he was badly beaten up in the tavern. Otis had done more than any other person at the time in the colony to achieve independence, but due to injuries sustained in this row, he was unable to partake in the struggle he ignited. The beating Otis received that night damaged his mind and lead to his withdrawal from public life.

As the Sons of Liberty increasingly controlled public space, King Street became overwhelmed with people gathering outside the British Coffee House. In this environment of anti-British sentiment the tavern changed its name. In 1792 the building was sold to house the Massachusetts Bank.

Bull, 1689, southwest corner of Summer and Federal streets. Landlords in succession: Bull, Bean and Bigelow. Bull's Wharf and Bull Lane were named after this tavern. English taverns were frequently called 'The Bull' after a license once issued by Catholic monks to operate a tavern on monastic lands. The license was called a Bulla (Latin for seal). The diverse inhabitants of the South End met here to plan a church on Church Green, called the "New South" Church. Demolished to make way for Atlantic Avenue in 1833. South Station stands on this site today.

Bull's Head, 1774, northeast corner of Congress and Water streets. Prior to 1830 the site hosted the Post Office, Merchants' Hall, and Topliff's Reading room. More recently occupied by the Massachusetts and Shawmut banks, and known as the Howe building.

Bunch of Grapes also **Coleman's,** 1712, southeast (later northwest) corner of State and Kilby streets. Hudson's tavern was originally on the same plot of land at the head of Long Wharf. Three gilded clusters of grapes dangled temptingly above the door. A portion of the sign that hung at the Bunch of Grapes, made of baked clay and said to have been imported from England, was displayed in the early 1900's at the Essex Institute, which merged with the Peabody Essex Museum in Salem. The museum cannot trace the whereabouts of the grapes today. The masons also cared for the grapes at one point in time, but they have no record of the current owners.

Figure 5: Bunch of Grapes, Cromwell's Head, Three Doves

Operated by Captain John Marston, previous owner of the Golden Ball, the Grapes was described as the "*best punch house in Boston*" Goelot, 1750. At that time the town dined at 2 o'clock daily and diner guests would be called together by the ringing of a bell in the street outside. They could expect salmon, veal, beef, mutton and fowl carved at the table, followed by a variety of puddings washed down with fine Madiera. Marston could accommodate a large number of guests judging from the 288 knives and forks he provided, with handles made of bone and ivory. Tea, brewed in an urn, was served in chinaware from silver teapots.

Marston, who became a Son of Liberty, was landlord here in 1775 until his death when his widow took over. In 1778 Marston was cautioned for allowing gambling, including backgammon. Marston's book collection indicates revolutionist ambitions, his library included literature on Oliver Cromwell, Russian czars, anti-English and Whig publications. The tavern evolved into a revolutionist hang out for the Sons of Liberty and a center for popular demonstration. Paul

Revere was commissioned by Marston and the other Sons of Liberty to produce an elaborate silver punch bowl in 1768. Inscriptions on the bowl describe people gathering in taverns to freely discuss matters of state and makes reference to several pieces of resistance literature. The bowl symbolizes not only the importance of punch drinking in the culture of the day, but also the role taverns were playing in the politics of Early America. Paul Revere's bowl was probably used more in the Bunch of Grapes tavern than any other place in Boston.

Several important events occurred here. George Washington was entertained in the Grapes. Some months later, after hearing the Declaration of Independence read from the town-house balcony, a mob pulled down royal arms displayed on public buildings all over Boston, then set them ablaze in front of the tavern. It was here that Governor John Hancock hosted a $1,000 dinner to put an end to the rivalry surrounding Pope Day, November 5th by inviting both parties to the table: the North and the South-enders. Each party had its own procession and its own pope effigy. When the two groups met—the borderline being Mill Bridge, Hanover Street—fists, sticks and stones were thrown until one of the rival popes was captured.

One of the most important events associated with this tavern is the founding of the Ohio Company here in 1876 by General Rufus Putnam. This event established the state of Ohio and began the movement of New England towards the Great West. By 1790 the tavern itself had moved to the west corner of State and Kilby streets. Noted as a brick store in 1798.

Castle also **George**, 1654, southwest corner of Dock Square and Elm Street. Built and operated by Lt. William Hudson Jr. previously from Hudson's House. Later kept by John Wing in 1687, who gave his name to the street. In 1694 it was called the George Tavern. In 1798, the aptly named Colonel Brewer was the occupier of this two-story brick house worth $4,000.

Castle 1654 also **King's Head,** 1785, northwest corner of North and Fleet streets.

Burnt and rebuilt in 1691. In 1755 kept by James Davenport, who was succeeded by his wife "*a maiden dwarf, fifty-two years old*"—an accomplishment at a stated height of 22 inches.

Cole's, 1633, southwest corner of Merchants Row and Corn Court, with an area in front on Merchants Row and also on Fanueil Hall Square. This is Boston's FIRST recorded ordinary.

Samuel Cole, comfit maker, set up the first house of common entertainment here in March, 1633. In 1635 he acquired a license for an ordinary. In 1636 Governor Vane invited Miantonimoh, the Narragansett Indian Chief to Boston and it was here that the party dined. The group probably sat on the floor of the tavern, as was their custom. In 1637 Cole sold his house to Robert Sedgwick.

James Penn took over in 1646. Lt. William Phelps sell the property now known as the "**Ship Tavern**" to Capt. Thomas Savage in 1660. In 1678 the landlord John Wing was accused of *"giving entertainment to other mens servants"* and fined 40 shillings. Laws existed to stop slaves and servants visiting taverns and consuming alcohol to the extent they were unfit for work. The Great Fire of 1711 started in the rear of the tavern. The tavern changed hands five times before James Lloyd acquired it in 1763 and kept it in his family for many years. Judge Sewall visited the Ship tavern with his Puritan Brothers to confront the, then landlord, Wing. Apparently Wing had *"set a Room in his House for a man to shew Tricks in"*. Sewall and his friends put a stop to the show by bursting into a sermon in the middle of the room, followed by a Psalm.

Commercial Coffee House, 1817, northeast corner of Milk and Batterymarch streets. Stood on the site of Hallowell's shipyard. In 1848 it ceased to be a public house, giving way to the Thorndike building. Apparently this was a favorite meeting spot for Eastern people.

City Tavern, later **City Hotel,** east side of Washington St. between State and Water streets. One of the most popular stagecoach inns.

Congress House, 1815, northeast corner of Pearl and High streets. Built as the mansion of Daniel Hammond in 1815. First kept as a public house in 1840 by Hastings. Destroyed in the great fire of November 8, 1872.

Concert Hall, 1750, southeast corner of Hanover and Court streets. The hall was used for meetings, parties, concerts and by the Grand Masons. A famous Belgian giant called Bihin exhibited himself here. Thomas Turner had a dancing and fencing academy here in 1776. The building became a tavern in 1791. Demolished in 1868 to widen Hanover Street.

Copp's, 1799, south side of City Sq., near the corner of Bow St. in Charlestown. In 1866 the building, which had not been a tavern for some time, was demolished to make way for Waverley House.

Cromwell's Head, 1764, no. 13 (north side) School St. The two-story wooden building had a large sign hanging outside of Oliver Cromwell, who revolted against the British Royal family. It was hung so low that people would cross the street to avoid walking under it. When the British soldiers put Boston under martial law, the landlord, Brackett, hid the sign. Members of the Brackett family kept the tavern for over half a century. This was the tavern of the gentry. An intelligent young Virginian named Colonel George Washington, said to be a good engineer and soldier, lodged here, while he discussed military matters with the then Governor Shirley. The tavern was advertised for sale in 1802. Apparently a Mrs. Harrington served her customers with coffee and mince pies from this building in 1884.

Cross 1709 also **Red Cross,** 1746, southwest corner of North and Cross streets. Cross St. acquired its name from the tavern. In 1729 Samuel Mattocks advertises two young bears "*very tame*" for sale at the "*Sign of the Cross*". Men who enlisted for the Canada expedition were ordered to report to here. The name originates from 'Cross Keys,' a popular name for English taverns, outside which a sign was displayed of crossed keys, symbolizing the power in Catholicism of the Keys.

Crown Coffee House, 1710, southwest corner of State Street and Chatham Row. The first house on Long Wharf, extended from State St. in 1710. Originally built by Gov. Belcher. Like most of these waterside taverns the owners would live upstairs, while the taproom and parlor included beds for guests. Standing at the head of Long wharf, and one of the first buildings in view of debarking passengers who crossed the Atlantic, the tavern was a popular place to gather news and refreshment. Thomas Selby, tavernkeeper from 1714-1725, modeled the tavern after English institutions and introduced the tastes of the English gentry to Bostonians. The tavern hosted luxurious gatherings for Boston's elite.

Thomas Selby, probably from England, was admitted as an inhabitant of the colony in 1709. He personified the style and elegance of the day, wearing a periwig in a society that earlier condemned such vanities. He owned an extensive wardrobe including silk garments, which indicates that most of the tavern work was performed by others, probably slaves. The tavern accommodated large parties called gentleman's clubs in its parlor, which contained fifty chairs, thirty-five of which were leather. The one thousand clay pipes that Selby held in inventory for sale indicates that this tavern was a very smoky place. Twenty brass candlesticks provided light inside. Two looking (perspective) glasses were available for the entertainment of his customers. Selby owned thirty books and a bible, a large amount of literature at that time.

The bar had "*sashes on each side*" with a copper coffee pot and coffee grinder in the corner. A coffee pot on a stand and two leather fire buckets stood by the fireplace. Despite the name of this tavern and the fact there was an entire room elaborately decorated and devoted to coffee consumption, Selby sold far more wine than coffee. Although coffee was fashionable, Selby owned over a thousand pounds worth of alcoholic drinks. Wine and rum were the taverns most popular drinks and Selby kept 1,760 bottles stacked in his yard, more than any other Boston tavern keeper. In addition to the popular Madeira and Canary wine, the Crown Coffee House offered Vidonia (a dry white wine from Tenerife), Fayall (a Portugese wine from the Azores) and Red Jury (possibly a French wine from Eastern France). Good quality rum and brandy was available along with a variety of limejuices. The Crown Coffee House brought cosmopolitan tastes from London to Puritan Boston. Mrs. Anna Swords rented the tavern and successfully catered to Boston's elite for nine years in the 1740's until she was evicted. By 1798 stores covered this location.

Dog and Pot, c.1722, North St. at head of Bartlett's Wharf.

Dolphin 1726, east side of North St. at the foot of Richmond St. In London taverns were often the meeting places of trade associations, in the case of watermen on the Thames they frequented a bar called the Dolphin. It is very likely that the Dolphin in Boston was named after the local watermen who visited it.

Doolittle's City Tavern, 1807, northwest corner of Washington and Brattle streets. Served as headquarters for the Providence line of stagecoaches. Demolished in 1874 during the expansion of Washington Street.

Dove, 1667, northeast corner of Boylston and Tremont streets.

Drum, 1761.

Eastern Stage House, 1806, No. 90 North St. Built on the same spot that the first stagecoach in America left from, in 1660, for Portsmouth (NH). Originally kept by Col. Ephraim Wildes, who was succeeded by his son, Moses. The stage house was a three-story brick construction with sixty rooms. Accommodating the stages to Portsmouth, Portland and Bangor, it was the most extensive stagecoach rendezvous in Boston. The stages entered its spacious courtyard under an arch leading from North Street. Around 1846 it was torn down to make way for commercial improvements.

Earl's Coffee House, 1807, No. 24 Hanover St. On the site of the American House. Its name came from the owner, Hezekiah Earl. Served as headquarters of the New York and Albany stagecoach lines.

Elm Street Hotel, 1812, northwest corner of Washington and No. 9 Elm St. Kept by Hart Davenport. It's yard was demolished in 1874 to make way for the Washington Street extension. In 1882 the building was removed for commercial purposes.

Exchange, 1697 also **Royal Exchange**, northwest corner of State and Exchange streets. A very successful tavern due to the market on its doorstep and being adjacent to a side street that went down to the docks. In 1708 Boston magistrates investigated "*debaucheries at the Exchange*". The result; one young man was fined for cursing, throwing a beer-pot at the maid and lying. It did not get much worse than that in these days. The original building was destroyed in the great fire of 1711 and replaced with a three-story brick structure. The Royal Exchange tavern gave its name to the street on its easterly side. This was where the young, wealthy and trendy could be found at night, drinking, gaming and recounting their love life. In 1728 two such local young men argued over their cards. A challenge was made. The weapon of gentlemen in those days was the sword. The men withdrew to Boston Common and fought in the moonlight until one of the men called Woodbridge took a fatal thrust. The survivor was hurried off to a ship by his friends, which immediately set sail. This was the first duel in Boston.

When the nearby townhouse burnt down in 1747, the General Court took residence here. In 1754 the building was known as the "Royal Exchange Tavern". The exchange was popular with the newly arrived British officers of the army and navy. On the frosty night of 5th March, 1770, a sentry was standing guard on the opposite corner of the tavern, in front of the Custom House. A mob taunted him until other British soldiers came to the sentry's support. A free-for-all then ensued and shots were fired into the crowd. The event went down in history as the Boston Massacre and is portrayed in Paul Revere's famous picture of the scene. The first stagecoaches to New York left from the Exchange. Israel Hatch kept the tavern in 1800. 28 State Street now occupies this site.

Exchange Coffee House 1808, Congress Square, southeast corner of State and Devonshire streets. Completed in 1808 from plans by Asher Benjamin. Extending through to Devonshire Street, with an entrance on State Street it held 132 feet on Congress Street, with a depth of 94 feet, covering an area of 12,753 square feet. The building had 210 apartments. Its construction took two and a half years. Standing 7 stories high with marble pilasters, a complex interior staircase, a vast dome (101 ft in diameter) and an impressive dining room that catered for three hundred people. At the time the coffee house was the largest house of public entertainment in the United States. Kept by Col. James Hamilton. The building was very prominent on the skyline of Boston. After only 10 years of operation it was burnt down in 1818 and not rebuilt until 1822, taking 3 years and costing $500,000. The result was a mammoth construction for its day—7 stories and 200 bedrooms. Designed to handle the stagecoach traffic that stopped here. The register of shipping news, arrivals and departures was stored in the coffeehouse. Kept by William Gallagher, Hart Davenport, and lastly by McGill & Fearing. In 1853 it was demolished and replaced by the City Exchange on Congress Square and Devonshire St.

Figure 6: The Exchange—courtesy of The Bostonian Society

Flower de Luce, 1675, west side of North St. between Union and Cross St.

Forster's Coffee House, 1817, corner of Court and Howard streets.

Franklin House, 1830, west side of Merchants Row, between North Market and North streets, opposite the start of Clinton St. An eminent merchant on Long Wharf called Joshua Sears lived here for many years.

George 1788, **St. George** 1701, also **King's Head**, northwest corner of Washington St. and Northampton St. near the Roxbury line. The George was a very popular name for taverns in England, in honor of the patron saint of England. Located on the "Neck" a thin strip of land with a road that connected Boston to the mainland. The tavern gave shelter to the patriots when annoying the British during their siege. Originally its large orchard and gardens consisted of seventeen acres, extending south to Roxbury Street and west to the Charles River. Prior to 1730 the tavern hosted the General Court and other law courts. In 1775 the American post was located there. The tavern occupied an unfortunate position in disputed territory during the siege of Boston. It was directly in the line of fire and protected by General Washington's Continental Army. On July 5th Washington and General Lee visited the tavern to view the British advance. On July 31st at 1am the British attacked by land and river. They set fire to the tavern and returned to their positions. After peace had been restored another tavern was erected on this site in 1788 called the "George". Kept by a woman named Sally Burton who hosted bull baiting for public entertainment.

Globe 1741, northeast corner of Commercial and Hanover streets.

Goat, 1737.

Golden Ball 1711, northwest corner of Merchants Row and Corn Court. The tavern acquired its name from a large golden ball that swung outside. Golden balls were normally hung outside the premises of London silk merchants. Kept by Captain John Marston from 1757 to 1775, after which he left to manage the Bunch of Grapes. Replaced by warehouses in 1795. The Golden Ball sign is in the possession of the Bostonian Society. The Golden Ball kept rolling…

1799 swinging in Elm St. for Nathan Winship.

1805 used as a hotel sign on Fourth Avenue.

1811 back on Elm St. at Joseph Bradley's tavern.

1816 hung outside Thomas Murphy's tavern on Congress St.

1833 swinging for Henry Cabot, ornamental painter.

Figure 7: Golden Ball sign—courtesy of The Bostonian Society

Golden Bull, 1693, southeast corner of Merchants Row and Chatham Street. Kept in 1752 by Marston. This tavern is likely to have been the Golden Ball above.

Good Woman, North End. The sign of the tavern bore the image of a headless woman. A pun based on the bloodthirsty Henry VIII, whom had his wife Anne Boleyn beheaded.

Grand Turk, Sign of 1789, formerly **Lion,** Washington St. between Winter and Boylston streets. Occupied by Israel Hatch, possibly Boston's most notorious tavern keeper; he also kept the White Horse in 1787, his own tavern called the Hatch in 1796 and the Exchange in 1798.

Green Dragon 1665, originally **Baker's Arms, Freemason's Arms,** 11 Marshal St. Boston's most famous tavern originally occupied two-thirds of an acre on Union St. Its hard to believe but boats docked feet away from where Union Street is today, in the center of city. The building was first used by Thomas Hawkins, baker, to land and store corn. In 1665 Hawkins was licensed for a house of entertainment. The tavern was known as the "*Baker's Arms*". Home brewing was traditionally completed alongside baking; being a baker it was easy for Hawkins to extend his business to include beer fermentation by constructing a brew-house. In 1657 John Cary was the proprietor, in 1675 William Staughton took over. Unfortunately on a cold December night in 1690 the Green Dragon was burnt to the ground Snow on the roofs of adjoining houses saved those buildings. Within a couple of years the tavern was rebuilt by Mr Stoughton, then changed hands to Mrs. Thomas in 1701. Ownership then continued (the following names are proudly displayed along the top of the bar today) Richard Pullen 1712, Dr. William Douglas 1753, John Simpson 1754, until the building was raised by fire in 1854.

It was in the Green Dragon where Samuel Adams and James Otis penned their complaints and resistance of the 1765 Stamp Act, a British tax imposed on taverns by making the owners purchase stamps (the British levied the tax to pay off debts accumulated from warring with France). The stamps were to be hung on the wall of each tavern in Boston. The Stamp Act was the first attempt at an official tavern licensing system.

The building was purchased in 1764 by St. Andrews Lodge. The Tavern was downstairs and the Grand Lodge of Massachusetts resided upstairs. The Green Dragon was the largest meeting place in northeast Boston and became known as "*headquarters of the American Revolution.*" Described as a "*nest of treason*" by the British, the Green Dragon was home for Paul Revere and thirty of his compatriots called the *"Revolution Club."* In 1771 they met here to share intelligence on the movements of British soldiers and Tories. It was from the Green Dragon that Paul Revere left for his famous horse-ride in 1775, to warn the volunteers in Lexington that British soldiers were coming. A veteran drummer, Daniel Sampson, was at one time its landlord. A tea urn from the tavern is currently kept in the State House in Boston.

Figure 8: Green Dragon's Tea Urn—courtesy of The Bostonian Society

Each room in the tavern was aptly named, such as the "*Cross Keys*" where a charitable society for Scottish immigrants met. The name arises from the fact that two members each had a key to the moneybox. There were also the *Rose & Sun Low Room, Anchor and Castle Chamber,* which all happened to be popular tavern names in England at that time. The most noted room was the *Green Dragon,* which is where the tavern gets its current name. Although there is an alternative story of how the tavern acquired its name: As most colonists could not read, taverns were marked with signs. The Dragon had a copper sculpture of a dragon above the door. The Boston climate corroded the dragon to a bright shade of green, faster than the owners could keep it polished. So the tavern became known as the "*Green Dragon*". The Green Dragon tavern you can see on Union Street today is sadly not the original. It was opened by John J Summers, the current proprietor in 1993. A plaque just outside the tavern commemorates the original building, demolished in the widening of Union Street.

Figure 9: The Green Dragon—courtesy of The Bostonian Society

The British plan to capture Sanm Adams and John Hancock, then seize the powder stored at Concord, Mass. was found at the Green Dragon tavern. A thirteen year old boy called Sam Ballard heard two British officers talking about the plan. He alerted the landlord who informed the relevant people in good time.

The Tea Party & The Dragon

The British were never able to identify who was involved in the Boston Tea Party. A picture was later discovered of the Green Dragon Tavern with these words below: "*Where we met to Plan the Consignment of a few Shiploads of Tea, Dec 16, 1773.*" A square and compass can be seen in the upper left hand corner, the sign of the Masons. Many of the dockworkers were masons and their HQ was the Green Dragon. This is what many believe happened on the night of the Boston Tea Party, December 16th, 1773:

Three British ships full of tea were moored in the harbor. The consignment couldn't be unloaded because the colonials refused to pay the tax imposed on them by their cash starved government in London. In disgust of the new British tax on tea, the Sons of Liberty had been holding secret sessions in the Green Dragon, planning the night for months. Sam Adams joined John Hancock at the tavern. Hancock funded several barrels of beer to the delight of the regulars as they arrived at the Dragon. The sons of Liberty blackened their faces with cork and put on their disguise, a poor imitation of Mohawk Indians, but enough to avoid being recognized. They left their tankards of ale and headed for the docks to unload three tea-laden ships. When the party ended, 342 broken chests floated in Boston harbor and 35,000 pounds of tea swirled in the saltwater. Boston harbor was turned into a giant teapot. After that day it was said that if a man ordered tea in Boston, he was a Tory. If he ordered coffee, he was a Patriot. The English claimed the reason the Americans lost their taste for tea was due to their peculiar way of mixing it with saltwater!

Gutteridge Coffee House 1691, north side of State St. between Washington and Exchange Street.

Half Moon 1705, southwest side of Portland St. or north-west corner of Fleet and Sun Court streets. Kept in 1752 by Deborah Chick.

Hancock House, also **Brasier Inn,** 1790, 1 Corn Street, between State Street and Fanuiel Hall Square. In 1790 John Duggan was granted a license to sell liquor from his two storey, four room, 12 window house. Governor Hancock never actually resided here. The landlord was an admirer of John Hancock and when he was elected to Governor of the commonwealth Duggan had the tavern sign painted with Hancock's portrait. An advertisement in the Columbian Centinel of October 11, 1794 reads: "*Latest imported lemons—In excellent order, for sale, by John Duggan, at his house, at the sign of Gov. Hancock outside the market.*" When Hancock died in 1793 Duggan hang mourning emblems on the tavern sign. Some time later, after swinging for years over the narrow alley beside the tavern, the sign was suddenly blown from its fastenings in a high wind, killing a passer by. When replaced, the sign was securely fastened to the side of the building. The tavern was demolished to make way for offices in 1903. The sign survived and was last spotted in the Memorial Hall in Lexington. The Lexington Historical Society are unaware of the signs whereabouts today.

Figure 10: Hancock House—courtesy of The Bostonian Society

Hat & Helmet, 1770, Newbury St.

Hatch c.1796, east side of Tremont St., between West and Boylston streets. Israel Hatch took ownership of the tavern in 1794. By 1796 he was recorded as the tavern keeper. After running several taverns in Boston he finally named one after himself.

Hawk c.1740, Summer St.

Holland's Coffee House 1800, Howard St., near Court St. Later known as **Howard Street House** and kept by William Gallagher, whose tomb at Primrose Path in Mt. Auburn reads *"erected by those connected with him by no tie of kindred, who knew, loved, and honored him"*. William was obviously a popular tavern keeper. After his death the tavern was called the **Pemberton House**. It was a favorite resort of literary, dramatic, and musical people. Destroyed by fire in 1854 and replaced for a short period of time by a wooden circular structure called Father Miller's Tabernacle. When this also burnt to the ground the Howard Athenaeum was constructed here.

Horse Shoe c.1722, east side of Tremont between School and Bromfield streets.

Hudson's House, 1640, southeast corner of State and Kilby streets. This is Boston's THIRD recorded ordinary. William Hudson, baker, had an easy transition to tavern keeper in 1640 (beer was often made alongside bread in early kitchens). His name appears on the list of those admitted as freemen of the Colony in 1631. Things looked a little different around Boston then; the tide flowed nearly up to the tavern door. Hudson's son, also called William, later took over the business. The Bunch of Grapes appeared on this same plot of land several years later.

Indian Chief. Charlestown. Built in 1779 as the mansion of David Wood, an influential citizen of Charlestown. On the second story there was a hall, known as the "Massachusetts Hall." David Starrett, cashier of the Hillsboro', N.H. Bank, was robbed and murdered here in the evening of March 26th, 1812. Samuel Gordon, the landlord stood accused of the crime. A $200 reward was announced for the recovery of the dead body, which was never found. In 1814 the Hon. Nathan Appleton received a letter from the apparently dead Starrett, now in South America, where he had fled. The tavern was moved in 1818 to the northwest corner of Main and Miller streets, where it was known as the **Eagle** Tavern. The Harvard Church occupied its previous site. The Eagle remained in business until 1860.

Ingersoll's on Tremont Street at Court Street; a plaque at this site reads—in 1789, President George Washington stayed at Joseph Ingersoll's inn at this site while visiting Boston. Massachusetts Governor John Hancock's visit to meet Washington here is regarded as an early acceptance of federal sovereignty over that of individual states. Daniel Webster would later have law offices here, and Boston grocer S.S. Pierce started a thriving and long-lived provisions business in 1831.

Ireland's 1797, north side of Cambridge St., near the Lowell railway bridge.

Julien Restorator c.1794, northwest corner of Milk and Congress streets. Originally a private dwelling that dated back to 1670. Named after its cook, Jean Baptiste Gilbert Payplat dis Julien, a refuge from the French Revolution. This was the first French restaurant in America, a gourmet experience so new that the locals couldn't pronounce it. Hence the term *restorator*, a poor attempt to turn the French word restaurant into English. Before then restaurants were simply known as *cook-shops*. Jean Baptiste was called the "*Prince of Soups*" as his famous soups preceded most meals. Miraculously Julien's restaurant survived the town fires of the 1760's. After Jean Baptiste died in 1805 his widow carried on the business on her own for another 10 years. The building was torn down to make way for Julien (later Congress) Hall in 1824.

Figure 11: Julien Restorator

King's Arms 1642, also **State's Arms**, west side of Washington Street, between Brattle and Court streets. Hugh Gunnison kept a *cooke's shop* in his house here well before he was allowed to sell beer in 1642. Inns in England frequently used the name King's Arms at this time. Puritan rulers subsequently ordered a change of name, but in 1666 it reverted back to its original royal title. Hugh sold the estate to Henry Shrimpton and others for $1,000 in 1651. At that time all the rooms had been named, including the 'Exchange' where merchants met, and the 'Court Chamber', frequently assigned to the General Court of Mass. when they met here. Other rooms included the 'London' and 'Star'. In 1721 Eliakim Hutchinson took ownership of the estate. He was a loyalist and the property was confiscated and conveyed by the government to others in 1782. The tavern once stood at the head of the docks. Now the site has been consumed by Washington Street itself.

King's Arms, 1656, west side of North St. between Sun Court and Fleet St.

King's Head, 1680, corner of North and Lewis streets. Burnt in 1691, then rebuilt. Kept by James Davenport in 1755. Taken down in 1870. There is an old story from England regarding the tavern's name: A King was dancing with a fair young damsel at a public court ball. One of the courtiers, wishing to retire to a tavern asked another what inn he would recommend. The reply was that he had better not go to the 'King's Arms,' as they were full, but that the 'King's Head' was empty.

Figure 12: Site of King's Head—courtesy of The Bostonian Society

King's Head, 1717, King's Street, just up from the Crown. In 1714 Boston selectmen admitted James Pitson, a cider maker from London, as an inhabitant of Boston and approved his petition to sell cider. The selectman believed that manufacturing cider in Boston would be beneficial to the town by reducing the demand for rum. James and his wife Hannah rented a shop from Governor William Drummer and operated the tavern with the assistance of a slave called Prince. Pitson provided seating for fifty-eight customers including twelve 'Turkey Work' chairs in the taproom. Pitson had silverware for thirty-six and wine glasses for eighteen. Although the cider maker kept more cider in stock than any other tavern at that time in Boston, Pitson had diversified from what the selectmen had hoped for, judging from the following inventory:

Cider (530 gallons), Madeira (12 gallons), Canary Wine (10 gallons), Sherry (17 bottles), West India and New England Rum (152 gallons), Brandy (9 gallons), Dock Stevens Beer (18 bottles), Bristol Beer, Bitter (2 bottles). The latter items likely to have been imported from England. The 432 empty bottles noted in the inventory at the King's Head suggests sales were good.

Pitson owned a coffee mill, but only provided two cups. Instead he preferred creating punch from his inventory of mint water (12 gallons) and clove water (10 gallons) in china bowls—the very best taverns had silver bowls. The cider maker sold the latest refinements in drinking etiquette such as glasses (sixty-six) and punch bowls (twenty-nine). Judging from the inventory and location, the King's Head catered to artisans, travelers and people from the countryside who knew how to use a fork and appreciated a tavern where drinks were served in glass.

Boston's First Library

Pitson owned eighty-eight books and thirty-one pamphlets, kept on a shelf behind his bar in the taproom. Considering the King's Head catered to people of lesser rank than other Boston taverns, the extent of the collection is impressive. Pitson proudly displayed literature to artisans and tradesmen, both locals and strangers, no doubt encouraging them to read items of social and political interest. It is probable that the King's Head is Boston's earliest lending library. People of low to middle rank could now enjoy news and opinion previous limited to Boston's elite. Authors were reaching an audience they never intended and possibly never wished to address.

Lafayette Hotel, 1825, east side of Washington Street, opposite Boylston market. A favorite stop for people from the country. Kept by Haskell in 1836.

Lamb, also known as **White Lamb,** 1746 north corner of Avery and Washington Street. A popular resort of the country members of the Legislature. The first stagecoach to Providence was accommodated here. The name came from its owner, Laban Adams, in whose honor the Adams House was constructed in 1846.

Figure 13: Lamb—courtesy of The Bostonian Society

Liberty Tree, 1833, southeast corner of Washington and Essex streets. The famous elm tree was planted in 1646. In 1765 The Sons of Liberty hung an effigy of the hated King's stamp collector on the old elm. The tree became known as the Liberty Tree and was cut down by the British in 1775. A Liberty Tree Tavern also existed in nearby Dorchester, where the Sons of Liberty frequently met.

Light House, 1717, south side of King (State) Street, on the northwest corner of Devonshire Street, opposite the Town House (now known as the Old State House).

Lighthouse and Anchor, 1763, near the Old North Meeting House. Catered to the local boatmen and dockworkers. In 1763 the "Portsmouth Flying Stage" started here every Saturday morning, carrying six passengers at a fare of $3.25 to Portsmouth or $2.17 to Newburyport. Returning from Portsmouth on Tuesdays.

Lion, Sign of 1796, Washington St., between Winter & Boylston streets. Stood not far from the Lamb Tavern. The sign bore an image of a lion. The Paramount Theatre now occupies this site.

From Taverns Came Theatres:

Boston's theatre district evolved from its taverns. Theatrical performances started around 1800 in the assembly hall at the Lion Tavern. This was Boston's first theatre. The Lion tavern was the only way station on the popular travel route where Washington and Tremont streets traversed the isthmus of land tying Boston to the mainland (called the Neck). Entertainment flourished here leading to the construction of Lion's Theatre nearby in 1836. This building is still standing and is now known as the Bijou Theatre. In 1882 the Bijou was the first theatre to show films commercially. It was also the first to install electric lighting.

Logwood Tree, Sign of 1734, south side of Commercial St. between Hanover and North streets.

Mansion House, 1835, south side of City Square and northwest corner of Warren Avenue in Charlestown. Built in 1780 as a mansion for the Hon. Thomas Russell. First used as a hotel in 1835. Kept by Gorham Bigelow, then by James Ramsay. Demolished in 1866 to make way for Waverley House.

Marlborough Arms 1640, also **Marlborough Head**, south side of State St. and east of Kilby St. Located close by the Bunch of Grapes. Named after the Duke of Marlborough. The Widow Wormall moved here from her tavern on Fish Street in the North End and kept the tavern from 1716-1721. Elizabeth Smith was the last recorded licensee in 1722. By 1798 it had been converted into a brick store.

Marlboro' Hotel, 1708, Marlborough St. The first public house in Boston dignified with the name of "Hotel." The business took its name from the street in front. A stable in the rear accommodated the stages to Providence. The stables became the site of the Lowell Institute building. Scientists such as Agassiz, Lyell, Tyndall, Price gave lectures there. Other famous speakers include John Quincy Adams, Daniel Webster, Edward Everett, Rufus Choate, Charles Sumner, Bayard Taylor, William Lloyd Garrison and James T. Fields. Lafayette was given a banquet at the Marlboro' upon his visit to Boston in 1824. During the temperance movement the hotel changed its name to the Marlboro' House. Hon. Henry Wilson, Vice-President of the United States, often frequented the hotel when in the city. The Hemenway building now occupies this site.

Massachusetts House, 1816, southwest corner of Endicott and Cross streets. A favorite spot for jockeys and others involved in horse racing.

Maverick House, 1835, Noddles or Williams Island. At the time the island had a handful of houses, a few factories and several garages. Made of wood, 94 feet long and 85 feet wide, six stories, containing eighty rooms. First landlord was

Major Jabez W. Barton. In 1841 C.M. Taft took over. The house, stables, and furniture were sold in 1842 for $62,500. The structure was demolished in 1845 to make way for other buildings including a hotel, houses, shops, and offices, until they were burnt down in 1857. A year later a new iron and brick building covered in mastic was completed by Mr. Sturtevant, standing 130 feet long on Maverick Square, with 180 rooms. It was known as the **Sturtevant House** for more than a decade before resuming its original title. A duel was held between Lieutenants Finch and White here in 1819. White tragically lost.

Mitre, east side of North St. between Sun Court and Fleet St. at the head of Hancock (Lewis) Wharf. The lot was described as formerly the Mitre tavern in 1782.

Mount Washington House, 1834, Washington Heights. In 1839 the owning company became bankrupt and sold the property to the Perkins Institute and New England Asylum for the Blind.

North Coffee House, 1702, North St.

North End Coffee-House, 1782, also **Philadelphia** northwest side of North St. between Sun Court and Fleet Street. Capt. David Porter licensed to keep the tavern in 1782. A sign from that time reads "*Lodges, clubs societies etc. may be provided with dinners and suppers,—small and retired rooms for small company,—oyster suppers in the nicest manner.*"

Old Mansion House, 1732, south side of Milk Street, between Hawley and Arch Streets. Standing a little back from the street than most taverns, characterized by several large American elms that stood in front. The Mansion House was a common stop for stages. The Bowdoin building later occupied the same site.

Orange Tree, 1678, northeast corner of Hanover and Court streets. Known for the best well water in town—never dry or frozen. Kept by Jonathan Wardwell, who in 1712, set up the first hackney-coach stand (taxi service) in Boston, located just outside the tavern. His widow kept the tavern in 1724. Demolished in 1785.

Page's, corner of Main and Gardner streets in Charlestown. Later known as **Richard's**, and then **Babcock's**. In 1828 the Charlestown hourly coaches left from here to Brattle Street in Boston. Passengers were gathered by calling their name in the tavern.

Peacock 1705, also **Turkie Cock**, west side of North St. between Board Alley and Cross St.

Pearl Street House, 1836, northwest corner of Milk and Pearl streets. Built in 1816 as the mansion of William Pratt. First landlord was Colonel Shepherd. Destroyed in the great fire of November 8th, 1872.

Peggy Moore's Boarding House, 1798, southwest corner of Washington and Boylston streets. A favorite stopover and place of business for country folk visiting Boston to sell their produce.

Perkins House, 1839, west side of Pearl Street, halfway between Milk and High streets. Originally built in 1815 as the mansion of Hon. Thomas H. Perkins, who later donated it to the Asylum for the Blind in 1833. In 1839 the institution moved to Mount Washington House and Perkins House opened. A Scotchman named Thomas Gordon was the first landlord. He was a member of the Scottish Charitable Society that frequently met here. Perkins House was renowned for good downtown dining. Closed in 1848, as more profitable commerce encroached on its doorstep.

Pierce's Hotel, northwest corner of Charles River Ave. and Water St. Built in 1795 as a mansion for the Hon. Thomas Russell and his family. Last kept by James Walker, and known as **Middlesex House**. Destroyed in the great fire of August 28th 1835.

Pine Tree, 1785, Dock Sq. First licensed by Capt. Benjamin Gorham.

Piper's, southwest corner of Main and Alford streets in Charlestown.

Punch Bowl, 1789, Dock Square. Mrs. Baker was the tavern keeper.

Queen's Head, 1691, northwest corner of North and Clark streets.

Red Lyon, 1654, northeast corner of North and Richmond streets. The oldest tavern in the North End. The tavern and brew house stood by the waterside, facing the Red Lion wharf on the corner of Red Lion Lane. The lane is now called Richmond St., the wharf has long been filled in and the waterside is much further away. Nicholas Upshall, a Quaker, owned the tavern. When his sect became persecuted, Upshall was outspoken enough to find himself imprisoned for life. Paul Revere carved and painted a sign for the Red Lyon. During the Revolution, signs with British figures or symbols (i.e. the Red Lion) became very unpopular and tavernkeepers took steps to alter their appearance. The keeper of one Red Lion tavern had an artist paint a furiously clawing game cock on the lion's back. The building that hosted the Red Lyon still existed in 1798 according to local records.

Rising Sun, Washington St. between School and Winter streets. In 1800 Luther Emes was the tavern keeper.

Robbin's, 1796, west side of City Square and southeast corner of Harvard Street in Charlestown. Located behind the Three Cranes Tavern. Demolished in 1816 to make way for the Charlestown Town Hall, which was demolished in 1868 to create City Hall.

Roebuck, 1650, east side of Merchants Row, between Clinton and North streets. Apparently built by a descendant of Richard (a.k.a. Dick) Whittington, the famous Lord Mayor of London. In 1776, it is noted as standing on the east side of Merchants' Row (Swing Bridge Lane) and licensed by Elizabeth

Wittington (another relative). This tavern had one of the worst reputations of all in Boston; playing host to at least one murder, which led to a hanging in 1817.

Roebuck, 1702, Battery March by the South Battery.

Rose and Crown, 1697, southwest corner of State and Devonshire streets. Now the site of the National Park Service's visitor center.

Salutation, 1662, known from 1757 as the **Two Palaverers,** northeast corner of North St. and Salutation Alley. This tavern appealed more to the 'common people' of the era; shipwrights, caulkers, gravers and spar-makers. Acting like a clan, they were very patriotic and disliked the wealthier classes. Shrewd politicians such as Samuel Adams understood voting power and would visit tavern meetings to get their support. The word "*caucus*" which means lively gathering (from caulkers) originates from these meetings. Apparently this was Paul Revere's favorite hang out according to Esther Forbes book on his life. The rebellious caucus continued until the Boston Tea Party, when the group moved to the Green Dragon for more secrecy.

The religious tavern name originates from a time in Britain when monasteries operated guesthouses for visitors; the Catholic Church was responsible for naming these early forms of taverns. The practice of borrowing tavern names from Britain still continues in Boston today; there is currently an English theme pub called the 'Elephant and Castle' (borrowed from a famous pub in London) and an Irish tavern named the 'Black Rose' (a common pub name in Ireland). The Salutation was later renamed the Two Palaverers by North Enders after its sign; a humorous image of two wealthy Bostonians bowing, with cocked hats and knee-breeches, saluting each other in an overtly polite manner.

Schooner in Distress and **Schooner,** 1761, North St. between Cross and Richmond streets. The signboard outside read: "*With sorrows I am compass'd round; Pray lend a hand my ship's aground.*"

Seven Stars, 1698, southwest corner of Summer and Hawley streets. The tavern gave its name to the road, later called Bishop's Alley. In 1728 ownership changed for $450 to John Barnes and others to make way for Trinity Church.

Shawmut House, 1831, north side of Hanover Street, later consumed by the American House.

Shakespeare, located on Water Street.

Ship, west side of North Street between Sun Court and Fleet Street. Building dates back to 1659.

Ship Tavern, later **Noah's Ark,** 1650, southwest corner of North and Clarke streets. Built by Captain Thomas Hawkins, whose shipyard was below, he was later lost at sea. Ship Street took its name from this tavern, which stood at the head of Clarke's Wharf; Boston's most prominent wharf of the time. The building had two story's (a third later added), with brick walls, overhanging eaves and roof with projecting Lutheran windows. The front wall had a crack from the 1663 earthquake. John Vyal was tavern keeper in 1663 and gave lodging to King Charles's commissioners who had come to bring the colonists back in line. By that time the tavern had become known as "*Noah's Ark*" due to the resemblance of the ship on its sign. The Noah's Ark was also the name given to pubs in London who catered for shipwrights. Beside the tavern Vyal had one of the first brew-houses in Boston, with an excellent reputation. The tavern was demolished in 1866.

Shippen's Crane, 1739, located at Dock Square.

Star Tavern, 1645, northeast corner of Hanover and Union streets. Originally kept by Thomas Hawkins, and then by Andrew Neal, a Scotchman. The landlord was a member of The Scots' Charitable Society, which held its meetings there. By 1737 it was converted back to a house.

Stackpole House 1823, northeast corner of Milk and Devonshire streets. Originally built in 1732, as the mansion of William Stackpole, a noted Boston merchant. First kept as a public house in 1823 by Rouillard, from the Julien House. This was a fashionable establishment. Among its last landlords was Alexander McGregor, a stalwart Scotchman. He was a descendant of Rev. James McGregor who founded a colony in Derry (NH) in 1824. McGregor was also a member of the Scots' Charitable Society, which frequently held its meetings here. Demolished in 1868 to accommodate the post-office building.

State Arms 1645, southeast corner of State and Exchange streets. Just before the revolution the tavern became occupied as the customhouse. This may be the tavern previously mentioned under 'King's Arms'.

Sun, Batterymarch Street. The signboard contained a gilded sun, with rays, and the inscription: "*The best Ale and Porter, Under the Sun.*"

Sun c.1694, southwest corner of Dock and Faneuil Hall squares. The Sun was an important tavern near the public docks; it had by far the greatest number of chairs for tavern patrons in Boston, a total of 93 in 1727. Kept by Samuel Mears in 1724, by Capt. James Day in 1753. Conveyed by Thomas Valentine in 1741 for $8,250; by Joseph Jackson in 1794 for $4,444; and by E. P. Arnold in 1865 for $20,000. The Sun tavern was headquarters for the British during their siege. Said to be the oldest remaining building in Boston during the late 1800's.

Figure 14: Site of the Sun—courtesy of The Bostonian Society

Sun (second of that name) c.1782, west side of Washington Street, between Brattle and Court streets.

Sun (third of that name) 1824, northwest corner of Batterymarch and Hamilton streets. Originally built in 1801 as the mansion of Benjamin Hallowell, who owned the shipyard opposite. Kept as a tavern in 1824 by Goodwich, then in 1841 by Capewell, when it ceased to be a public house. The building was demolished in 1865 during the leveling of Fort Hill. Noted as a popular gathering place of people from the Far East.

Swan, 1707, northeast corner of North and Fleet streets. Known as **Queen's Head** in 1728.

Three Crowns, c.1718, North St. between Cross and Richmond streets.

Three Doves, 1759, Washington St. William Blair Townsend was the tavern keeper.

Three Horse Shoes, c. 1744, west side of Washington Street between School and Bromfield streets. The Three Horse Shoes is a reference to an emblem of a London livery—The Blacksmiths' Company.

Three Mariners, c.1679, later **Bear,** 1723 and **Bite,** 1800's, south side of Faneuil Hall Square.

Three Cranes, 1635, City Square, opposite the Waverley House and the base of the Town Hill, Charlestown. Before the settlers left England they ordered a building to be constructed to serve as a home for Governor Winthrop, along with other important community leaders, and to provide a religious and administrative office for the new colony. Then known as the "Great House." Due to the poor water supply and mosquito infestations in Charlestown the colony moved its center across the Charles River to the Shawmut Peninsula, to become what is now known as Boston. Some of the settlers remained in Charlestown and used the Great House as their meetinghouse for court-hearings and public worship. In 1635 a new meetinghouse was planned, so the Great House was abandoned and later sold to Robert Long, an Englishman from Dunstable in Great Britain. Long paid £30 for the lot. The property housed his family, which included 10 children and his new business, simply known as **Long's Ordinary**. The pilgrims imposed several restrictions on his ordinary: No tobacco, card-playing or dice throwing was allowed. The guests' horses could be kept in the pasture, but only if he fenced it. A fine of ten shillings would be levied for selling meals above sixpence or taking more than a "*penny for an ale-quart of beer out of meal-times.*" Selling cake or buns would receive the same fine unless there was a funeral, marriage, or similar occasion.

Robert's son, John, made several additions to the tavern before he died in 1683. These included a stable for visitors' horses and a brew-house to remove the brewing process from the kitchen (to the joy of the cook). A wine cellar was created under the Great House, which was raised on to a stone foundation. John built a new house for his family, connected to the main tavern, which freed up rooms for guests to rent in the tavern. In 1711, the estate now called the **Great Tavern**, was deeded by a Mrs. Long to her son Samuel. He later sold in 1712 to Ebenezer Breed, the house then known as the **Old Tavern**.

The tavern was destroyed by fire in the burning of Charlestown, during the battle of Bunker Hill on June 17th, 1775. By this time the building was known as the **Three Cranes Tavern** and had been open for 140 years. It was an established and successful business, popular with local patriots plotting against the British across the river in Boston. It would have been a rowdy atmosphere inside in its last days, with toasts to the American fight for freedom and curses to the British parliament, followed by the banging of firing glasses. The town of Charlestown later acquired the land, which now forms part of City Square.

Big Dig Update: Three Crane Tavern

Recently the area was excavated as part of the Big Dig (Boston's Central Artery construction project) and findings were plentiful. Patrons had dropped coins, buckles, and musket balls into privies during their stays. It is believed that patriots gathered there to plot events leading up to the Battle of Bunker Hill, the unusually large number of musket balls found by archeologists suggest the role it may have played in the events of that day. Stoneware jugs from the local Parker-Harris pottery were also found in the privies along with fragile porcelain tea bowls, delicate dessert glasses, fine tableware and wine glasses that date back to 1590. This suggests that tavern customers enjoyed a sophisticated lifestyle enhanced by trade with Germany, France, Holland, Spain, Italy, and the Far East. All this in the face of Navigation Acts imposed by the British, forbidding trade with whatever country the colonials might be at war with at the time. According to the Archaeological Data Recovery report for City Square, the tavern was probably a small two-story building with a kitchen on the ground floor, a slightly larger hall heated by a central fireplace, and a porch. Today you can see the tavern's foundation stones, preserved in their original location at City Square.

Tremont House, 1829—1832. Owned by William H. Eliot, brother of the mayor of Boston 1837-1840. One of the most prestigious hotels in Boston, hosting many renowned people including Daniel Webster on his way from Marshfield to Washington. President Jackson stopped here on his visit to Boston in 1833. President Tyler and President Johnson also stayed here. Charles Dickens patronized the Tremont House during his first visit to America in 1842. The Ashburton treaty, defining the north-eastern boundary between the United States and Great Britain, was negotiated here by Lord Ashburton for Great Britain, Abbott Lawrence for Massachusetts, and Edward Kent for Maine.

Union Flag, 1731, Battery March.

Union Oyster House, 1826, 40 Union Street. This is America's oldest operating restaurant. The original building is over 330 years old. The tavern is made of brick with small paned windows facing the street at obtuse angles. Upstairs the original fireplace and beams can still be seen. The top floor hosted the "*Massachusetts Spy,*" a patriot newspaper published from 1771 to 1775. The Duc d'Orleans stayed here in 1796-1800 during his exile from France. To generate money he provided French language and dancing lessons to fashionable ladies in town. During the Civil War, women made bandages and dressings for wounded soldiers here. Thomas Capen, importer of silks and fancy dress had a shop downstairs named *"At The Sign of the Cornfields."* In 1826 the building became an oyster bar; boats could deliver fresh shellfish to the back door. The maze of tiny streets that developed by the tavern over time; Old Creek Square, Marsh Lane, Creek Lane and Salt Lane provide an indication of how close the sea was in colonial times. Today you can sit at the original mahogany bar or in wooden booths and enjoy washing down oysters with a hot toddy, just as Daniel Webster did in his day.

Figure 15: Union Oyster House

Vernon's Head, also **Admiral Vernon,** c.1743, northeast corner of State St. and Merchants Row. The tavern sign bore a portrait of Admiral Edward Vernon, who was well known as *"Old Grog"*. Taverns, especially those at the waterside were fruitful places for navy recruiters. During the war with France, in 1745, the following notice appeared: *"All gentlemen sailors and others, who are minded to go on a cruise off of Cape Breton, on board the brigantine Hawk, Captain Phillip Bass commander, mounting fourteen carriage, and twenty swivel guns, going in consort with the brigantine Ranger, Captain Edward Fryer, commander of the like force, to* *intercept the East India, South Sea and other ships bound to Cape Breton, let them repair to the Widow Gray's at the Crown Tavern, at the head of Clark's Wharf, to go with Captain Bass, or to the Vernon's Head, Richard Smith's, in King Street, to go in the Ranger.*" As would-be sailors arrived at these taverns, drink would be made freely available to further encourage the potential recruits. Taverns catering to seafarers were often the scenes of brawls, in 1772 John Adams diary reads "*The Gunner and Captain's Clerk of the [ship] Beaver were drinking together at Admiral Vernon's Tavern; being warm'd with Liquor they quarell'd, when ye former stabbed ye latter with a stiletto…*" Simply providing sailors with rum and beer was a successful enough business plan for many dockside taverns known as '*tippling houses*', '*grog shops*' or '*slop shops*'. Such grog shops became renowned for illegally selling liquor under the counter to apprentices and servants as well. By 1798 Vernon's tavern had become a brick store.

Warren Tavern, 1780, 2 Pleasant Street on the corner of Warren Street, Charlestown. 617-241-8142. First kept by Eliphalet Newell. America's first Masonic lodge was founded here. The original sign bore a likeness of General Joseph Warren in his Masonic insignia as Grand Master of the lodge. Paul Revere was a close friend and stated this was his favorite tavern. He regularly attended the lodge meetings presided over by his close friend General Warren. The General was killed in the battle of Bunker Hill fought nearby. George Washington visited in 1789. A meeting hall was later added to the rear of the tavern, shown in the picture below. Today you can still indulge in unpretentious tavern fare, including real ale, in what is probably the most authentic tavern in Boston.

Figure 16: Warren Tavern

Washington Hotel, 1809, Broomfield Street. Later known as **Indian Queen** (the sign outside bore an image of an Indian princess). Later known as **Bromfield House**. Last kept by Selden Crockett.

Washington Hotel, 1819, northwest corner of Washington Street and Worcester Place.

Washington House, 1820, built on the site of Washington market, on the southwest corner of Washington and Lenox streets. A favorite gathering place for sleighing parties. Kept by Messrs. Cooley.

White Bear, 1757.

White Horse, c.1700, northwest corner of Washington and Boylston streets. The earlier mentioned Israel Hatch was licensed here in 1787.

White Horse, 1789, Cambridge St. near Charles River Bridge.

Wilde's, 1807, northeast corner of Washington and Elm streets. Demolished in 1874 during the Washington street extension.

Wolfe Tavern, near Faneuil Hall. General Wolfe was a favorite name and figure for pre-revolutionary taverns and signboards. These images of British officers were removed well before the Declaration of Independence, along with other tavern signs such as the "King's Arms," "King's Head," "St. George" and the "Dragon." Other British symbols also gave way to American eagles.

Yoelin's 1821, east side of City Square and northwest corner of Chamber Street in Charlestown. The building dated to 1798. The owners of Warren Bridge held their first meeting here in 1828. Destroyed in the great fire of August 28th, 1835.

Boston Taverns Today

THE number of remaining taverns in the city of Boston from the 1700's is precisely zero. However, the following establishments are linked to earlier houses of entertainment in various ways and are by definition Boston's most significant examples of local tavern heritage. As such they should be treasured and preserved as reminders of a bygone era. The background and history of each tavern is described in the 'A-Z List of Boston Taverns: 1630-1800' section of this book, with the exception of Jacob Wirth's which, in comparison, is a relative newcomer:

Three Cranes Tavern, 1635 (foundations preserved)
The Green Dragon, 1680 (in name only, close to its original location)
Warren Tavern, 1780 (original building)
Bell in Hand, 1795 (in name only)
Union Oyster House, 1826 (building dates to 1670's)
Jacob Wirth's, 1868 (oldest continuously-operated bar in Boston)

In addition, plaques noting the locations and historical significance of Ingersoll's and the Bunch of Grapes can be seen on Boston Streets today.

Hidden History Behind Bars

Moving from the past to the present, this section explores some little known hidden history behind existing bars in Boston today…

Boston's rich Irish heritage can be sampled hands-on in its thriving Irish bar scene. A relatively authentic Gaelic experience complete with regular live music and stout beer can be had at the **Black Rose**, 160 State St. and **Kitty O'Shea's**, in the old Board of Trade Building just up the road. Kitty O'Shea's takes its name from the married Katherine Parnell who is remembered for triggering Irish independence. The owners have hauled across the pond a diverse collection of antique Irish objects for display. Including an old church pulpit, a fireplace from a Georgian house in Dublin and stain glass windows showing scenes from around Ireland.

Figure 17: Kitty O'Shea's

Boston boasts an abundance of Irish bars around town. The reason is due to Boston's large Irish community and due to the fact that the winning hospitality formula travels well outside their homeland. The Irish have adopted beer drinking and bar culture as a national pastime, perfecting the art of serving beer while making a stranger feel like they are at home wherever they may be. One of the newest Irish bars in Boston is **Emmet's**, 6 Beacon Street, named after the famous Irish reformist. Emmet's succeeds in looking as if it's been there for centuries. Adjourned with traditional tavern decor it offers a more upscale Irish tavern experience.

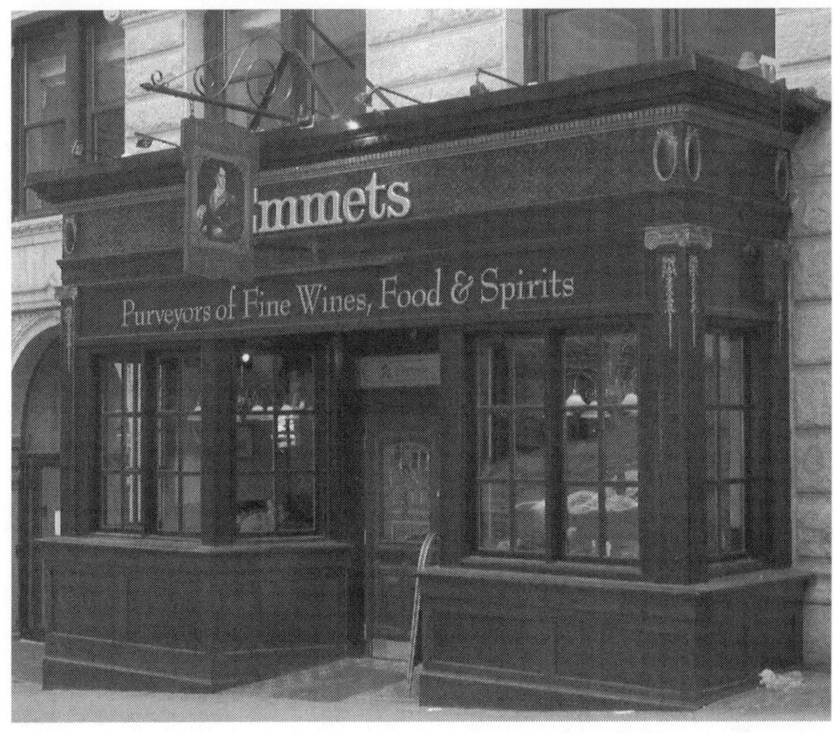

Figure 18: Emmet's

McGann's takes its name from the site it occupies, once known as Tommy McGann Square. Offering superb Irish breakfasts, its also a good source for Corn Beef and Cabbage around Saint Patrick's Day. **Red Hat**, 9 Bowdoin St., (617) 523-2175 is very proud of its location; pictures adjourning its walls depict Scollay's Square, before it was obliterated in the widening of Cambridge Street, to make way for Government Center in the 1960's. Established in 1903, Red Hat is now a very typical American basement bar.

Figure 19: Red Hat

Jacob Wirth's, (617) 338-8586 oozes with antiquity. Established in 1868, the business moved across the road to 37 Stuart Street in 1878. Jacob Wirth's Prussian upbringing was reflected in his menu featuring sausages, pig's knuckles, boiled bacon, hams, cheeses and herrings. The main room had simple mahogany tables, plus a few large steins and bottles for decoration. The floor was once covered with sawdust, now considered a fire hazard. Above the long mahogany bar a Latin motto proclaimed SUUM CUIQCE, meaning "Each his own." The business survived prohibition and anti-German sentiments of the two World Wars. Jacob, along with 5 other German-Americans, also founded the Narragansett Brewery in Rhode Island in 1890. Today the bar's exterior has been restored to look exactly as it did when Jacob opened it. This is Boston's oldest continuously operated tavern.

Figure 20: Jacob Wirth's—Then & Now

Wally's Café 427 Mass. Ave., (617) 423-0300, offers live jazz 365 days a year. Both big names and newcomers from Berklee College congregate at **Wally's** in the South End. Established in 1947, Wally was the first African American to own a nightclub in New England. In 1979 Wally closed his original location at 428 Massachusetts Ave and moved across the street to 427 Massachusetts Ave, where the bar remains today. Little has changed in its interior since the day it opened. Joseph L. Walcott, founder, passed away March 20, 1998 after a long and fruitful life.

Figure 21: Founder of Wally's Bar

The closest you can get to a real English pub is **Cornwall's**. Complete with traditional food and imported beers, the bar also displays a fine assortment of old tavern memorabilia. Guess the names of key British historical figures in the gigantic hand painted mural on the wall. The **Plough & Stars**, a little further out of town at 912 Mass. Ave. (617) 441-3455, is worthy of mention for the fact that it has changed little since the 1960's. The wooden bar, etched mirrors, battered tables and chairs create a classic tavern atmosphere reminiscent of many taverns of yesteryear. As the place fills with the artsy Harvard crowd, the conversation's get more animated and it's amazing how many bands manage to fit their amps into this small room. Expect to squeeze past the performers just to reach the bathroom. The Plough & Stars is living proof that the success of a tavern lies in its customers and service and not in its fixtures and fittings.

Bukowski's, 50 Dalton St. (617) 437-9999, is one of the few places in Boston that goes by the name of "Tavern". It's long and narrow, looks like a bowling alley and clings to the side of a big concrete car park beside the Mass Pike highway. Wonderful views of the passing traffic are available to patrons. Attracting a slightly younger and diverse crowd, the atmosphere is very laid back. If you are wondering why there are 175 mugs with dead authors names etched onto them hanging over the bar, then read on. The walls are covered in samples of the cult writer, Charles Bukowski's, alcohol induced work. They only have a license to sell beer or wine but they make up for it in the selection available—the only place where you can get Fuller's ESB from England on tap or a half liter of authentic German Hefeweizen. If you are undecided then spin the wheel of indecision and allow fate to choose. Just hope that it does not land on Schlitz, a beer with probably the worst reputation for taste and quality in the whole of America. To get your hands on one of those mugs you will have to spin the wheel many more times, in fact you need to sample all 100 bottles, plus the 15 beers on tap. After that you are entitled to your very own mug, and a refill if you're still thirsty. You don't have to accomplish this feat in one session. No credit, no problem; cash only here.

Space is limited at the **Littlest Bar** in Boston, (617) 523-9766. Look carefully near 47 Province St. to find this tiny tavern that's been here since 1945.

Figure 22: The Littlest Bar in Bean Town

In Boston today you can find bars in banks and even a police station. **Dillon's,** 955 Boylston St., (617) 421-1818, is a modern Irish bar residing in the old police station on Boylston. Likewise, **Jury's** (617) 266 7200 is located in the cells of Boston's former Police HQ at 350 Stuart St., a 1920's architectural landmark in Boston's Back Bay. The ultra modern **Mantra**, 52 Temple Place, (617) 542-8111 once hosted one of the grandest banks in Boston. Upstairs you'll find a cavernous interior and downstairs you can walk through the old steel lined vaults and combination doors on your way to the most advanced yet confusing men's room in Boston (you'll find out why). This Indian themed bar/restaurant on Temple Place transforms into a heaving nightspot at the weekends. It's hard to imagine that cashiers and bank staff once conducted their daily business here. Likewise **McFadden's** at 148 State Street (617) 227-5100 has a cavernous downstairs; as you go through iron bar doors you can sip your drink securely amongst safety deposit boxes from a bygone era.

Hotel bars have always been a popular hang out in Boston. The Park Plaza Hotel boasts **Whiskey Park**, a trendy bar for the cool crowd. The Copley Plaza

Hotel has the **Oak Bar**, a classy lounge with jazz, cigars and specialty martinis. The Lenox Hotel on Boylston hosts **City Bar**, offering signature cocktails and premium spirits. On top of the new Ritz Carlton Hotel, by the Common, is **Blu**, which provides an aerial view of the old leather district. Below the Copley Square Hotel is **Saint**, a contradiction in itself providing a futuristic yet overtly old-fashioned experience. You are greeted with glowing pillars and stainless steel mirrors in the all-white lobby and vodka bar, called the Threshold Room. In contrast is the adjacent Bordello Room, dimly lit, offering leather sofas to lounge on and admire paintings inspired by women of the 1940's. The **Top of The Hub**, 800 Boylston Place, (617) 536-1775 is located at the top of the Prudential Tower and is also at the top of many visitors' to-do lists. Renowned for its views, the Top of the Hub offers a 360° birds' eye view of the city.

Coogan's Bluff, 173 Milk St., (617) 451-7415, occupies a classic federal style building constructed in 1805 to rejuvenate the downtown area and promote maritime trade.

Figure 23: Coogan's Bluff

Aptly named, **The Point** at 147 Hanover St., 617-527-0988, occupies what has to be one of the narrowest buildings in Boston. Located on the doorstep of the old Haymarket, still held in the street outside on Saturday mornings. Continuing Boston's tradition of inviting and entertaining tavern signs is **Bakey's**, 45 Broad St. (617) 426-1710. They should win a prize for their inventiveness and creativity in warning city workers of the hazards of lunchtime drinking.

Figure 24: Bakey's & Cheers signs

In terms of fame, one bar stands out from the rest. Tourists flock to the **Bull & Finch** or '**Cheers**' bar, at 84 Beacon St. 617 227 9605. Established in 1895. Despite what most people think the famous TV sitcom was not filmed here, the bar merely formed the inspiration for the series.

Authentic Taverns Near Boston

NEW England offers the weary traveler several authentic period taverns. The inns listed here offer the closest experience you can receive to colonial taverns today. They are all original; you can drink, dine and sleep in the same places as characters in this book, such as our old friend Judge Sewall, who visited these establishments while completing his circuit hundreds of years' prior.

Longfellow's Wayside Inn, 1716. 77 Inn Road, off Rte. 20. South Sudbury, MASSACHUSSETTS. This is the oldest operating tavern in Massachusetts. Originally known as Howe's Tavern after its owner David Howe. The original structure had just two rooms, one above the other. It was kept in the Howe family for many generations. Longfellow visited in 1862, and based his book "*Tales of a Wayside Inn*" on a group of fictitious characters that regularly gathered at the tavern. Longfellow's immortal phrase "*listen my children and you shall hear, of the midnight ride of Paul Revere*" had Lyman Howe in mind as the character featured in "*The Landlord's Tale.*" After being owned by Henry Ford, the inn was turned into a non-profit. Every attempt is made to create a realistic 18th century experience; oil lanterns light your way to the inn from the gravel drive that was once the Boston Post Road. You can even board your animals in the barn. If you stay the night ask for room 9 or 10 above the old kitchen, they are the most historic. www.wayside.org

Buckman Tavern, 1710. Lexington Common at 1 Bedford Street, MASSACHUSETTS. On April 19, 1775, Captain Parker's company of minutemen left their headquarters at John Buckman's tavern to assemble in two long lines on the common. The British arrived and a shot was fired that sparked the beginning of the American Revolution. The Buckman Tavern in its central location was convenient for both churchgoers and for drovers bringing their cattle to market, making it the busiest in town during its heyday of the 1700's. The Lexington Historical Society has restored the interior to how it looked in 1775. During their 1920's restoration, the original seven foot-wide taproom fireplace was unearthed and the bar reinstalled. Look out for the original front door, with a bullet hole from a British musket fired during the Battle, and a portrait of the then owner, John Buckman. www.lexingtonhistory.org

Monroe Tavern, 1696. One mile east of Lexington Common, MASSACHUSETTS. On April 19, 1775, the British occupied the tavern for one and a half hours as headquarters for Brigadier General Earl Percy and his one thousand reinforcements. The dining room was converted into a field hospital while the British soldiers helped themselves to food and drink. A bullet hole can still be seen in the taproom ceiling. The tavern is named after William Munroe, a sergeant of Captain Parker's minuteman company in 1775 and tavern owner from 1770 to 1827. The eighteenth century tavern sign along with other family articles are on display. President Washington dined here when visiting the Lexington battlefield in 1789. You can see the table at which he sat upstairs. www.lexingtonhistory.org

Hartwell Tavern, 1733. Battle Road, Concord, MASSACHUSETTS. Built and managed by Ephraim and Elizabeth Hartwell as a tavern and farmhouse.

Located near the infamous "bloody angle" where British soldiers were caught in a bloody crossfire during their retreat from Lexington Common. The tavern is possibly the most authentic in New England. In 1965 the building was acquired by the National Park Service who completely restored the interior and exterior to the day the British marched past; April 17th, 1775. The building is open during normal park hours. No food or refreshments are available but it's a great place to wander around and get a feel for 1700's tavern life. Points of interest include the sparingly decorated interior, dimly lit rooms, the brick central fireplace in the taproom and the original exposed beams. The wooden furniture is authentically basic and practical which adds to the rustic character of the tavern. Costume interpreters are on hand to teach visitors about the daily lives of the Hartwells and their guests. www.nps.gov/mima/pphtml/facilities.html

Golden Ball Tavern, 1768, 662 Boston Post Road, Weston, MASSACHUSETTS 781-894-1751. Home of the prominent 18th century Westonian Isaac Jones. The tavern "at the sign of the golden ball" operated as an inn from 1770 to 1793 for travelers on the Boston Post Road. After 1793, for six generations (200 years) it was occupied by the same family, until being acquired by the Golden Ball Tavern Trust in the 1960's. Most of the furnishings, including pictures, ceramics, silver, glass, textiles and furniture, belonged to the Jones family. The trust has even gone to the trouble of recreating earthenware pitchers and wallpaper based on samples found on site. Tours by appointment only, events held annually, check online at www.goldenballtavern.org.

Old Ordinary, Hingham, MASSACHUSETTS 781-749-7721. A 17th-century building that began as a home, and eventually became a tavern serving ordinary fare and warming drink to its customers, is currently a house museum owned and operated by the Hingham Historical Society. www.hinghamhistorical.org

Hancock Inn, 1789. 33 Main St., Hancock, NEW HAMPSHIRE. Stay in one of the lavish historically preserved rooms, once used by cattle drovers, rumrunners, sleigh riders, the aristocracy, a U.S. president and the first riders of the Boston and Maine railroad. The Rufus Porter Room is adjourned in murals painted by an artist in return for food and board. On the way for Bostonians going to northern Vermont, the inn was renowned for its elegant grand balls and dancing in a room lit by tallow-candle chandeliers. Guests were served whole roasts of turkey, goose and beef from open fires until the first 'modern' cook stove was installed in 1857. www.hancockinn.com

Ye Olde Tavern, 1790. 5183 Main St., Manchester Center, VERMONT. Dorset master builder Aaron Sheldon, built the spring floor in its third floor ballroom and the distinguishing high square columns on its porch. Known as the Stagecoach Inn, it was founded when Vermont was still an independent republic. A pineapple motif, the colonial symbol of hospitality, is proudly displayed on the front door knocker. Great food is served in the fireplace illuminated taproom. www.yeoldetavern.net

White Horse Tavern, 1673. 26 Marlborough St., Newport, RHODE ISLAND. In 1687, Mayes, father of a notorious pirate who returned to Newport with treasures from the Red Sea, acquired a tavern license. The townspeople welcomed the pirate and his loot, to the annoyance of the local British rulers. The pirate succeeded his father as tavern keeper. In 1730, Jonathan Nichols became the taverns owner and named it the White Horse Tavern. His son, the tavern keeper in 1776, moved his family out rather than live under the same roof as the British 'Hessian' mercenaries who had moved in by force. After the war, Nichols came back, reopened the tavern and added the gambrel roof plus the addition. This barn shaped building now offers upscale colonial fare for dinner. www.whitehorsetavern.com

Randall's Ordinary, 1790. 41 Norwich Westerly Road, Rte. 2, North Stonington, CONNECTICUT. The existing building was built by John Randall in 1680 and stayed in the family as a farm for over two hundred years. The Randalls were one of the first to free their slaves. In the Keep (Hearth Room), there is a trap door that leads to a secret room where freed slaves were hidden. Today food is cooked hearthside in the tavern and servers appear in 17th century dress. www.randallsordinary.com

Boston Brewing

From Alewives to Breweries

THE first breweries in Boston, although small in number, were very successful businesses and could barely keep up with this demand. Originally, alewives home brewed much of the ale available in the early 1600's. As taverns emerged, they often brewed their own beer or relied on imports from Britain. As a major colonial trade center, there was a heavy demand for beer in Boston from ships stocking up on refreshments for their next journey. In 1711 a crisis occurred due to a shortage of imported barley. Panic buying quickly diminished local supplies and Bostonians took action; a large group prevented one Boston merchant's shipment of barley from leaving the harbor. With beer a major part of colonial diets, a disruption of beer supply was affected most inhabitants. Despite these shortages, Boston was slow to learn its lesson, with the advent of war with England, the supply of both barley and beer was in jeopardy. Keeping local troops healthy and happy during the war effort that ensued made local beer production critical to the independence of America. So important that securing beer supply became a military objective for both sides. Revolutionary War measures made by Congress in 1775 included rationing one quart of Spruce Beer or Cider per soldier per day.

It was not until 1789 that the Massachusetts authorities took beer supply seriously, when George Washington delivered his "Buy American" campaign. In which he stated he would only drink porter (his favorite beer) if made in America. Bostonians jumped on the "Buy American" bandwagon by passing an Act to *"encourage the manufacture and consumption of strong beer, ale and other malt liquors."* Boston later became a Mecca for beer production in America during the 1800's. Scores of breweries boomed in the industrial age resulting in hundreds of craft brews. At this time the creation of commercially produced ice improved the lagering of beer and later the steam engine automated production in the brewery. Between 1870 and 1890 some 22 new breweries were constructed, by 1890 Boston was home to 27 breweries in total. Then came prohibition.

Notable Boston Brewers

The most notorious brewers in Boston from 1630-1830 include:

Captain Robert Sedgwick. Mr. Robert Sedgwick, chosen as Captain for Charlestown, was promptly issued the first license to brew beer for the Colony. The licensing seems like a bit of a formality seeing he had already set up a brewery and had been brewing for some time.

Seth Perry. During 1685-89 Perry is credited with supplying the ketch Endeavor with 7 barrels and the brigantine Robert with 6. He also supplied barley in bushels to home brewers, of which there were many among the citizens of the time.

Sampson Salter. Born in Boston in 1692, by 1730 he had become Boston's leading brewer. Expanding beyond the local market by partnering with Peter Faneuil (a successful merchant who financed Faneuil Hall) to supply ships in the harbor. Sales ledgers of the time from the wharves in Boston reveal frequent sales from Salter's Leveretts Lane brewery.

Robert Whately. He adopted the same strategy of Salter to become another of Boston's famous brewers. **John Carey**, who started his operation on Cambridge Street in 1710 was another popular brewer. Sea Captains such as **Nathaniel Oliver** started constructing their own breweries on Water Street to supply their ships.

John Cooper and **Thomas Gould.** They built a small brick building in Charleston, 1821, near where 40 Alford Street stands today, with varied success at brewing. In the same spot **John Kent** established Mystic Lake Brewery, evolving into a four-story brick building with a stone cellar. In 1860 **William Van Nostrand** bought a stake of this brewery and steadily expanded production and distribution. The brewery was responsible for "*P.B. Ale*"—Boston's favorite beer at one time. In fact it was so popular that less reputable retailers would sell other beers on draft under the name P.B. Ale. The brewery later became known as **Bunker Hill Brewery** and thrived, gaining the title of America's oldest continually operated brewery until finally becoming a victim of the Massachusetts Prohibition in 1919.

In South Boston the **Boston Beer Company** opened in 1828. By brewing non-alcoholic beverages during the prohibition it took the record for the oldest operating brewery in America until 1957. Unable to keep up with Bostonian's new taste for lager, the South Boston dinosaur, after 129 years of continuous operation, was forced to give up its title.

Stony Brook: HQ of Boston Brewing

After 1830 many of Boston's early breweries were located along the Stony Brook corridor in Roxbury's Mission Hill neighborhood. The location was conducive to brewing due to the low price of land, a skilled local German community and nearby water supply from Stony Brook itself. Brewing became Boston's sixth largest industry by the 1890's. Stony Brook hosted 22 of the 31 breweries in Boston in 1900, but their success was short lived. Prohibition wiped out Boston's brewing industry, leading to widespread destruction of these structures in the third quarter of the twentieth century. The only brewery still in operation today is the Haffenreffer Brewery, revived by the Boston Beer Company (see below). Some of these old breweries in Stony Brook made Preservation Mass.'s 2003 Ten Most Endangered Historic Resources list. The Friends of Historic Mission Hill is working to make the brewery complexes a thematic National Register Historic District. Although not open to the public, the buildings are: **Vienna Brewery/Carl Jutz Brewery/A.J. Houghton Brewery** (1870) at 37 Station Street and 133 Halleck Street, **Eblana Brewery/John Alley Brewery** (1885) at 117, 123-125 Heath Street, **Highland Spring Brewery/Croft Brewery** (1867) at 166-168 and 158-166 Terrace Street, **American Brewing Company** (1891) at 251 Heath Street and **Roxbury Brewing Company** (1896) at 31 Heath Street.

What's Brewing Today?

The colonists drank beer in the morning for breakfast alongside bread and cheese, with their lunchtime meal and with leftovers on which they "supped" in the evening. To taste a similar beer today you will need to brew it yourself. It's not easy, but the taste sensation and experience itself is well worth the effort. There are several recipes contained in this book, but the best approach is to use a local self-brewery known as a brew on premises operation. There are two places near Boston; Barleycorn in Natick, MA (508) 651-8885 www.barleycorn.com and Deja-Brew in Shrewsbury, MA (508) 842-8991 www.deja-brew.com. Ask for a nut-brown ale recipe, with a relatively low alcohol %, slightly sweet, low carbonation. The real thing would have also been cask conditioned. The only problem is that this authentic beer will go flat within a couple of days, and go sour within a week. Brewing a 5-gallon batch for a party is fine, but if you intend to consume the ale mostly by yourself it may go bad before you finish drinking it. Once the serving cask is tapped, air gets to the beer and causes it to go flat and stale quickly. Air is not beer's best friend; the puritans didn't allow their beer to hang around for too long and neither should you. Early colonials used bread yeast; they had little other choice. You don't get a very good beer from bread yeast so its best avoided.

If you're used to drinking bland national beers, then the first sip of these self-brews will come as a revelation. They are so smooth and flavorful that you may find it difficult to crack open a can of Bud or Old Milwaukee again.

If you haven't got the time to brew authentic nut brown ale then the next best thing is to try some of these local equivalents; Beantown Nut Brown Ale (Boston Beerworks), Ipswich Nut Brown Ale (Mercury Brewing Company), Wachusett Nut Brown Ale (Wachusett Brewing Company). At the time of writing Hyland's Brewery is planning to brew a brown ale for Old Sturbridge Village in Western Mass., which promises to be one of the most authentic ales available locally.

Brewing in Boston has gone full circle; modern brewpubs are reminiscent of the 1600's when beer was brewed locally in taverns as opposed to the large commercial breweries that dominated the1900's. The growing number of craft brewers in Massachusetts remind us of the 1700's when production was characterized by a large number of small local breweries. Today similarly sized American brew operations are going back to their roots, creating fresher, more robust ales. Craft brewed lagers are becoming complex, malty, and rich in flavor. A new generation of craft brewers are producing increasingly more variety of fine lagers and ales, with a multitude of ingredients, reminiscent of the experimental periods of the 1600-1700's. Today close to fifteen craft breweries of different sizes exist in the Greater Boston area, the most popular are listed here:

Samuel Adams Brewery (Boston Beer Company), 30 Germania St. 617-368-5080. www.samueladams.com. In 1748, after receiving his degree from Harvard University, Samuel Adams, a simply dressed, austere young man, inherited his family's malt house. However Sam was a better brewer of dissent than of beer; as his revolutionary ambitions grew, the business fell apart, after the British left Boston nothing remained on Adams' South End property near Fort Point Channel.

The association between Sam Adams and brewing in Boston today is a creation of a young management consultant in 1984. Jim Koch came from a family of many successful brewers. He transferred his forefather's famous lager recipe from its St. Louis home to Boston and established the Sam Adams brewery on the disused site of the Haffenreffer brewery. Don't be fooled into thinking that the Sam Adams beer you drink is actually brewed in Boston. They just perform the research and development locally and outsource production to larger commercial breweries. There are few pictures of the original Sam Adams in existence, so Jim Koch commissioned an artist to create the Sam Adams we see all over Boston on beer advertisements today. The artist created the image from a statue of Sam outside Fanuiel Hall. Over the last few years you may have noticed Sam's smile has got bigger and his glass has got higher! Call the brewery for details of the superb tour and generous sampling opportunity.

Figure 25: Sam Adams—Then & Now—courtesy of Boston Brewing Company

Harpoon Brewery, 306 Northern Ave., 617-574-9551. www. harpoon brewery.com. Upon receiving the first permit to be issued in 25 years by the Commonwealth of Massachusetts to brew and package beer commercially, the Harpoon Brewery began brewing in 1987. Call for details of the free brewery tour and sampling. Harpoon are locally renowned for their IPA.

Boston Beer Works, 61 Brookline Ave., 617-536-2337 also 112 Canal Street. A brew pub that performs tours and tasting for a small donation to charity. Started by two brothers, Steve and Joe, by 1993 The Slesar Bros. Brewing Co. gained national prominence by producing the largest number of barrels of any brewpub in America. Walk in any day of the week to sample 4 beers of your choice in 4 oz glasses. Try the blueberry ale, containing whole blueberries.

Rock Bottom, 115 Stuart Street, Boston, 617-742-2739. www.rockbottom.com. Fresh, handcrafted beers brewed on premise ranging in style from an IPA and Light

Lager to a Gold and Amber Ale. Plus many specialty and seasonal beers, crafted from the Brewmaster Gerry O'Connell's original recipes.

Cambridge Brewing Company, 1 Kendall Square, Cambridge 617-494-1994. www.cambrew.com. Founded in 1989, the Cambridge Brewing Company is one of the original brewery—restaurants in Boston. Serving beer in a refurbished mill building in the heart of high-tech and bio-tech Kendall Square.

John Harvard's Brew House, 33 Dunster Street, Cambridge 617-868-3585. www.johnharvards.com. Real beer in an English style pub setting. Voted Brewpub of the Year by the Improper Bostonian.

For more information on what's brewing today visit www.beeradvocate.com and Yankee Brew News, New England's Beeriodical, which can be picked up at many of the businesses listed here.

AFTERWORD

Due to the tremendous support the author has received from others in the local historical preservation and brewing communities, a range of services are now available to help educate others and preserve old taverns, including:

- Advice for taverns wishing to replicate the atmosphere, drinks and culture of tavern life in the 1600-1800's.
- Recipes for authentic colonial drinks and food menu design.
- A library of hard to find books and articles on early American taverns.
- Architectural and structural engineering services to help in the preservation and restoration of early taverns.
- Guided walking tours of Boston's historic taverns, then and now.

Please contact the author at oldtaverns@hotmail.com

EPILOGUE

If this book achieves just one thing, it should be in demonstrating the importance of Boston's tavern heritage; major historical events in Boston are intrinsically linked to local taverns. For this reason alone, extra effort should be made to preserve what's left of Boston's rich tavern history. Local sites on the endangered list include the foundations of the Three Cranes Tavern; the Green Dragon, Ingersoll's and the Bunch of Grapes wall plaques; the establishments now known as the Warren Tavern, Union Oyster House, and Jacob Wirth's. For their role in more recent history, notable bars include the Bull & Finch (of the TV series 'Cheers' fame), Plough & Stars (simply due to its lack of refurbishment in decades) and Wally's bar (important in terms of black history and culture) should be added to the endangered list.

Unfortunately, over the years many taverns have closed or changed their use; history tells us that if we don't use them—we'll lose them. Please support the education and preservation of early American taverns by telling others about this book.

Cheers.

About the Author

Gavin R. Nathan is a self-described "tavern connoisseur". While living in England, he developed a passion for old taverns, exploring and patronizing the old inns of London for 20 years and becoming an avid collector of breweriana. After moving to America, Gavin began a quest to unearth the history behind Boston's taverns. The author is a firm believer in primary research; every single recipe recommended for food and drink was self-tested. Likewise every remaining tavern and brewery mentioned in this book was personally sampled. As the author says "It's a dirty job, but someone's got to do it." Today Gavin considers Boston's tavern heritage crucial in understanding early colonial history. Gavin takes every opportunity to promote and preserve Boston's tavern heritage from advising local taverns on authenticity to various speaking engagements.

You can contact the author at oldtaverns@hotmail.com

Selected Bibliography

Balfour, David M. "Taverns of Boston in Ye Olden Time", The Bay State monthly, Volume 2, Issue 2; November 1884, pp. 106-120

Best, Michael R, "Introduction to The English Housewife", Mc-Gill-Queen's University Press, 1986.

Bonner, John, "The Town of Boston in New England", map dated 1722.

Conroy, David, "In Public Houses" 1995.

Drake and Watkins, "Old Boston Taverns and Tavern Clubs" 1917.

Drake, Samuel Adams, "Old Landmarks and Historic Personages of Boston" 1906.

Earle, Alice Morse, "Stage Coach and Tavern Days" 1900.

Field, Edward, "The Colonial Tavern: A glimpse of New England Town Life in the 17th and 18th centuries" 1897.

Forbes, Esther, "Paul Revere and The World He Lived In." Houghton, Mifflin & Co. 1969.

Glasse, Hannah, "The Art of Cooking Made Plain & Easy" 1745.

Haas, Irvin, "Americas Historic Inns and Taverns" 1972.

Kay, Jane Holtz, "Lost Boston" 1980.

Lathrop, Elise, "Early American Inns and Taverns" 1926.

Lender & Martin, "Drinking in America" 1987.

Mears, Samuel, Inventory of, Suffolk County Probate Records, Record Book, XXVII, 269

Marston, John, Suffolk County Probate Records, Record Book, LXXXVI, 12

Mather, Increase "Wo to Drunkards" 1673

Marlowe, George Francis, "Coaching Roads of New England" 1945.

McNulty, Elizabeth, "Boston Then and Now" 1999.

Pitson, James, Suffolk County Probate Records, Record Book, XXXIV, 360-364

Rice, Kym S., "Early American Taverns: for the Entertainment of Friends and Strangers"1983.

Selby, Thomas, Suffolk County Probate Records, Record Book, XXV, 530-555 and XIV 72-76

Yazawa, Mel, "Diary and Life of Samuel Sewall" 1998.

Simmons, Amelia, "The First American Cookbook" 1796

Index of Bars, Breweries and Notable Characters

978-0-595-39370-1
0-595-39370-5

12077587R00086

Made in the USA
Lexington, KY
21 November 2011